11+ Verbal Reasoning

For **GL** Assessment

When it comes to the 11+, getting top marks is key — and this CGP Stretch book is packed with extra-tricky questions to help pupils aged 10-11 master the hardest parts of the test.

It starts with a section of challenging questions for each topic, so children can practise each question type. Then, there's a selection of mixed-topic Assessment Tests where they can work on really polishing their exam technique.

We've also included detailed, step-by-step answers. Everything you need!

Stretch Practice Book
Ages 10-11

with Assessment Tests

How to use this Practice Book

This book is divided into two parts — themed question practice and full-length assessment tests. There are answers and detailed explanations at the back of the book.

Themed question practice

- Each page contains practice questions divided by topic. Use these pages to work out your child's strengths and the areas they find tricky. The questions get harder down each page.

- Particularly hard questions will be marked up with a green box around the question number.

- Your child can use the smiley face tick boxes to evaluate how confident they feel with each topic.

Assessment tests

- The second part of the book contains three full-length assessment tests, each with a mix of question types from the first half of the book. They take a similar form to the real test.

- You can print multiple-choice answer sheets so your child can practise the tests as if they're sitting the real thing — visit cgpbooks.co.uk/11plus/answer-sheets or scan the QR code. →

- Use the printable answer sheets if you want your child to do each test more than once.

- If you want to give your child timed practice, give them a time limit of 60 minutes for each test, and ask them to work as quickly and carefully as they can.

- Tests 1-3 get progressively harder, so your child will probably find the later ones more challenging.

- If they haven't managed to finish the test in time, they need to work on increasing their speed, whereas if they have made a lot of mistakes, they may need to work more carefully.

- Keep track of your child's scores using the progress chart on page 78.

Published by CGP

Editors:
Rachel Craig-McFeely, Robbie Driscoll, Becca Lakin, James Summersgill, Kirsty Sweetman, Matt Topping

With thanks to Andy Cashmore for the proofreading.
With thanks to Alice Dent for the copyright research.

ISBN: 978 1 78908 978 3

Printed by Elanders Ltd, Newcastle upon Tyne.
Clipart from Corel®

Based on the classic CGP style created by Richard Parsons.

Contents

Tick off the check box for each topic as you go along.

Missing Letters

Find the letter that will finish the first word and start the second word of each pair. The same letter must be used for both pairs.

Look at this example:

suc (?) it   as (?) oof   __h__   (**such**, **hit**, **ash** and **hoof**.)

1. to (?) we   ag (?) dd   _____

2. mas (?) iss   cas (?) ose   _____

3. ou (?) oad   dee (?) ank   _____

4. swa (?) old   com (?) oss   _____

5. her (?) ats   di (?) ven   _____

6. hoo (?) ust   gol (?) oes   _____

7. te (?) nd   gal (?) el   _____

 / 7

8. wi (?) ot   ra (?) uy   _____

9. rai (?) awn   rea (?) oot   _____

10. hu (?) row   jo (?) ulk   _____

11. pas (?) ue   plu (?) igh   _____

12. sil (?) ilt   as (?) ind   _____

13. hi (?) et   wa (?) uch   _____

14. run (?) own   win (?) rip   _____

/ 7

15. san (?) id   cor (?) one   _____

16. pat (?) ire   wis (?) ail   _____

17. wee (?) ill   ste (?) eep   _____

18. tri (?) ath   pol (?) at   _____

19. an (?) our   ba (?) elp   _____

20. bea (?) ook   pai (?) ews   _____

/ 6

 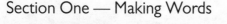

Missing Letters

Find the letter that will finish the first word and start the second word of each pair. The same letter must be used for both pairs.

1. hal (?) end   dea (?) ry   _____
2. tie (?) at   ai (?) ice   _____
3. fai (?) ose   woo (?) ift   _____
4. den (?) ell   tin (?) owl   _____
5. ble (?) ove   ja (?) aft   _____
6. swa (?) ap   rai (?) igh   _____
7. soa (?) osy   see (?) ind   _____

/ 7

8. bee (?) it   cal (?) ix   _____
9. ha (?) eal   mos (?) aid   _____
10. ar (?) ar   dis (?) ow   _____
11. goa (?) ish   wil (?) in   _____
12. wan (?) ye   lam (?) arn   _____
13. whe (?) our   foo (?) ank   _____
14. pa (?) ry   sho (?) ord   _____

/ 7

15. hea (?) ap   mus (?) ub   _____
16. war (?) our   swa (?) ave   _____
17. sou (?) est   ear (?) ain   _____
18. chi (?) ape   zin (?) ook   _____
19. cla (?) oe   wa (?) ire   _____
20. ski (?) ull   loo (?) use   _____
21. wai (?) awn   ree (?) eel   _____
22. spa (?) ag   moo (?) aut   _____

/ 8

Move a Letter

Remove one letter from the first word and add it to the second word to make two new words. Do not change the order of the other letters. Write the letter that moves on the line.

Look at this example:

| basis | sad | __i__ | (The new words are **bass** and **said**.) |

1. surge   fro   _____

2. chain   wit   _____

3. point   son   _____

4. swing   all   _____

5. charm   who   _____

6. suite   last   _____

7. speed   rely   _____

Hint: Watch out for questions where more than one letter could be removed from the first word — only one of these letters can be added to the second word.

/ 7

8. world   pain   _____

9. swift   seer   _____

10. chief   plot   _____

11. split   four   _____

12. reign   tier   _____

13. broad   reel   _____

14. front   apt   _____

/ 7

15. force   aid   _____

16. stand   vial   _____

17. carve   gray   _____

18. please   send   _____

19. cream   sore   _____

20. theme   ties   _____

/ 6

Section One — Making Words

Move a Letter

Remove one letter from the first word and add it to the second word to make two new words. Do not change the order of the other letters. Write the letter that moves on the line.

1. replay   raid   _____
2. range   sprig   _____
3. thrust   tough   _____
4. fairly   fight   _____
5. refuse   lair   _____
6. create   carer   _____
7. pitch   baked   _____

/ 7

8. write   blow   _____
9. about   lunch   _____
10. jaunt   ford   _____
11. friend   petty   _____
12. canyon   hone   _____
13. design   pent   _____
14. guild   debt   _____

/ 7

15. stage   face   _____
16. driver   seen   _____
17. rifle   deer   _____
18. avoid   curt   _____
19. spark   lined   _____
20. woven   gap   _____
21. blend   corer   _____
22. brain   pose   _____

/ 8

Section One — Making Words

6

Hidden Word

In each sentence below, a four-letter word is hidden at the end of one word and at the start of the next. Underline the part of the sentence that contains the hidden word and write the hidden word on the line.

Look at this example:

Will there <u>be an</u>y pizza at the party?   bean

1. She spat her words out furiously. _____

2. This flower will attract some bees. _____

3. The fish felt ripples in the water. _____

4. Every good soldier must follow orders. _____

5. A dragon could slay entire armies. _____

6. Stop the ribbon edge from fraying. _____

7. My third story is about a wizard. _____

/ 7

8. Some people ski with their own gear. _____

9. All flights were grounded due to the snow. _____

10. There is a bronze statue in the courtyard. _____

11. Maude spilt the black ink everywhere. _____

12. I dolloped the cream onto the fresh fruit. _____

13. The video mentioned both of their names. _____

14. My mum fixes watches in her workshop. _____

/ 7

15. Your gecko escaped and now I cannot find it. _____

16. My favourite bird is the beautiful snowy owl. _____

17. The zoo is known for its rather hyper kangaroos. _____

18. The system it created was actually rather helpful. _____

19. The winding path was lined with elm trees. _____

20. Boiling lava leaked from the rumbling volcano. _____

/ 6

Section One — Making Words

Hidden Word

In each sentence below, a four-letter word is hidden at the end of one word and at the start of the next. Underline the part of the sentence that contains the hidden word and write the hidden word on the line.

1. The cinema ultimately decided to close down. _____
2. You must give yourself little breaks when revising. _____
3. I wonder who axed such a famous programme. _____
4. That man sells huge amounts of gourmet cheese. _____
5. You can visit actual llamas at the farm. _____
6. A midge bothered us all night long. _____
7. Check it is dry before applying more paint. _____

/ 7

8. Nobody else could fit through the gap either. _____
9. Mia saw rye loaves in that bakery yesterday. _____
10. They saw him leave the supermarket ten minutes ago. _____
11. I have to buy myself a pair of trainers. _____
12. We clapped at the skilled circus performers. _____
13. Milo uttered an amusing joke about cats. _____
14. A spindly tree was growing within a crevice. _____

/ 7

15. The vigil tomorrow is an opportunity to mourn. _____
16. He bid everyone goodnight as the broadcast finished. _____
17. Our craft markets normally occur twice a month. _____
18. The forum aims to support anyone experiencing problems. _____
19. You stand silently before you are called. _____
20. I was glad my speech was met by a happy reaction. _____
21. A group of minstrels were playing lutes alongside flutes. _____
22. All audience members must turn off their devices. _____

/ 8

Section One — Making Words

Find the Missing Word

Find the three-letter word that completes the word in capital letters, and so finishes the sentence in a sensible way.
Write your answer on the line.

Look at this example.

| The mountain **RES** mission was a success. | CUE |

1. Please fetch the cough mixture from the medicine **CAET**. _____

2. I picked up a greyish **PLE** and threw it into the sea. _____

3. My flat has lots of **MRN** amenities, like a dishwasher. _____

4. We **ADED** a cat and her kittens from the local shelter. _____

5. The **MIUS** can seat a maximum of 12 passengers. _____

6. There was a **STAL** chandelier hanging from the ceiling. _____

7. You'll have to walk **SIAYS** through the gap in the rock. _____

/ 7

8. Yan started to get **FIDY** after sitting still for five minutes. _____

9. The room's **LAT** is odd — there is a sofa next to the bath. _____

10. An annual pass will offer you free entry to the **MUM**. _____

11. The team of archaeologists **EXCAED** the ancient temple. _____

12. Give our wonderful performers **AHER** round of applause. _____

13. The stormy beach is littered with tangles of green **SEED**. _____

14. **ROSEY** is a popular herb used in cooking. _____

/ 7

15. They couldn't resist stroking their rabbit's **VELY** ears. _____

16. The artist carefully mixed two colours on her **PATE**. _____

17. Sequins on the fabric **SMER** when they catch the light. _____

18. The pastry was shaped into a **LATT** on top of the filling. _____

19. My parents looked at our sodden puppy with **DISBEF**. _____

20. Spain's warm climate makes it **DEABLE** to tourists. _____

/ 6

Find the Missing Word

Find the three-letter word that completes the word in capital letters, and so finishes the sentence in a sensible way.
Write your answer on the line.

1. The car broke down due to a mechanical **MALCTION**. _____

2. The small, **STISH** bird flew away when I approached. _____

3. I **ASED** food would be provided, but I was disappointed. _____

4. The bullies apologised to everyone for acting **UNDLY**. _____

5. The atmosphere was **SUBD** after Ian broke the sad news. _____

6. Gran's **EIGHT** has worsened — she needs new glasses. _____

7. If we don't round up the sheep soon, chaos will **EN**. _____

/ 7

8. The soldiers feared their **HLESS** leader. _____

9. **NOAYS**, it is rare to see a horse-drawn carriage. _____

10. Several polished **AMEST** stones adorned the chest. _____

11. I didn't mean to **OVEACT** by screaming in your face. _____

12. **MARAN** can be sculpted into sweets or used in baking. _____

13. Though Ed's opinion differed, he respected her **JUDENT**. _____

14. All **PUCE**, from peas to pears, comes from our garden. _____

/ 7

15. The wizard **FORE** the wicked monster from returning. _____

16. Taj wondered what the author's metaphor was **IMING**. _____

17. The **PREVING** wind moved in a southwesterly direction. _____

18. Genevieve sneakily wiped the stain with a **SERTTE**. _____

19. I found the horror film extremely **HARROG** to watch. _____

20. He had an amazing **AFITY** with the area he grew up in. _____

21. Louisa's **QUY** designs are iconic in the fashion world. _____

22. The three intrepid adventurers began their **ARUS** ascent. _____

/ 8

Use a Rule to Make a Word

The words in the second set follow the same pattern as the words in the first set. Find the missing word to complete the second set.

Look at this example:

> ashy (shed) deny   make (_akin_) nine

1. nice (epic) pain   meld (_____) undo
2. daze (faze) fade   lash (_____) edge
3. sweat (anew) raven   storm (_____) apple
4. able (blue) fuel   whet (_____) polo
5. raft (farm) army   sock (_____) rile
6. piper (grip) fling   sinew (_____) dials
7. ramps (palm) local   stern (_____) flair

/ 7

8. floor (wore) wrote   anvil (_____) tacit
9. nope (open) pony   blew (_____) able
10. vets (vest) save   hike (_____) naps
11. grey (gore) ogre   nits (_____) nuts
12. lame (male) calm   shut (_____) flaw
13. iron (ring) grin   went (_____) taxi
14. cuts (cats) cast   flux (_____) wavy

/ 7

15. apron (pour) usurp   older (_____) brags
16. filed (fine) infer   gripe (_____) gawky
17. clown (cowl) allow   tower (_____) leach
18. idyll (laid) dial   homes (_____) bunk
19. maims (same) tease   worse (_____) eject
20. racer (cart) actor   final (_____) steep

/ 6

Use a Rule to Make a Word

> The words in the second set follow the same pattern as the words in the first set. Find the missing word to complete the second set.

1. renew (wear) awake   talon (_____) pixie

2. spool (clop) local   amuse (_____) wider

3. amaze (haze) ahead   baker (_____) irked

4. waded (awed) swear   canal (_____) avoid

5. llama (balm) bomb   alien (_____) lank

6. rail (liar) flair   bell (_____) agree

7. sees (seat) teas   hymn (_____) newt

/ 7

8. rowdy (word) drown   crept (_____) false

9. weir (wire) wiser   zest (_____) woman

10. dared (bead) babe   duvet (_____) goal

11. reheat (here) echo   impact (_____) toga

12. motto (omit) timid   murky (_____) cloth

13. zigzag (gaze) agenda   garlic (_____) camera

14. accord (coal) collar   peruse (_____) cement

15. skis (kiss) kits   avid (_____) tomb

/ 8

16. addle (deal) ladle   larva (_____) debts

17. access (case) ceases   legion (_____) fringe

18. edited (tide) tidied   reason (_____) opaque

19. appeal (peal) paella   occupy (_____) barrow

20. eerier (ride) deride   impale (_____) combat

21. masses (seam) sesame   vermin (_____) adores

22. prep (peeps) seep   lope (_____) lack

/ 7

Compound Words

Underline a word from the first set, followed by a word from the second set, that go together to form a new word.

Look at this example:

(plaque hung <u>bar</u>)   (ate rear <u>gain</u>)   (The word is **bargain**.)

1. (infant inhabit age)   (isle tries ants)

2. (bun loves awe)   (truck gallows sick)

3. (all sore miss)   (guide owing locate)

4. (wave toot worth)   (tall heir ring)

5. (cons bush treat)   (shell tables mint)

6. (enthrall enable equal)   (tee led lies)

7. (sand weigh feud)   (list dale tier)

/ 7

8. (bran imp fill)   (dish lament pose)

9. (prone den host)   (tell ounce aisle)

10. (sat decor err)   (us orates ant)

11. (deaf off serve)   (ice vile fend)

12. (mass tray fall)   (tours able aged)

13. (hear shows brew)   (stopping trending wing)

14. (ember suck grim)   (aced our oiled)

/ 7

15. (with feat seas)   (ores hers old)

16. (defer add read)   (all acts just)

17. (art port but)   (rail facts toning)

18. (clear deter jazz)   (mine rest rinse)

19. (crumb bare top)   (led rock pull)

20. (hone past close)   (set sty year)

/ 6

Compound Words

Underline a word from the first set, followed by a word from the second set, that go together to form a new word.

1. (serve not end)   (earring thing iced)

2. (rid spin tend)   (stir dance dull)

3. (stead come invest)   (dies gate stable)

4. (grave prop verb)   (hose tea ally)

5. (rein tram command)   (dear meld spire)

6. (tang both us)   (goes ability herd)

7. (dab herb garb)   (bled ill list)

/ 7

8. (peck kind gibe)   (red king liar)

9. (the mini rest)   (one mall rein)

10. (short thirst has)   (ten test tear)

11. (heart poor ear)   (shun then take)

12. (diver scar whim)   (city sly purr)

13. (engulf fur hall)   (nice fed owed)

14. (perm add reap)   (mitt eating apt)

15. (hum do disc)   (mane used bull)

/ 8

16. (doctor temper lace)   (oral rate ring)

17. (lit pastor seat)   (rally lest he)

18. (ten pare flag)   (rant gone drills)

19. (fat sip hand)   (sum full homed)

20. (tin can are)   (dour able cell)

21. (sole pall squall)   (lid or ace)

22. (pen bar sever)   (chant all rely)

/ 7

Section One — Making Words

Complete a Word Pair

> Find the word that completes the third pair of words so that it follows the same pattern as the first two pairs.
>
> Look at this example:

| script pit | caviar air | talent ___net___ |

1. brook broom   cover covet   sheen _____
2. rearrange are   urbanised bad   refashion _____
3. eligible lie   ridicule ice   suburban _____
4. vein vain   stun spun   clap _____
5. lifeline fin   caginess gas   category _____
6. spamming imp   strolled lot   beanpole _____
7. teammate mat   wieldier dew   emulsive _____

/ 7

8. character car   stratagem arm   crusading _____
9. kinking inn   craning ran   ability _____
10. rippling pip   flattery tea   reassert _____
11. elliptic lit   catholic ail   boulders _____
12. condemned den   gargoyles gel   paramedic _____
13. sequences use   exchanged hex   attending _____
14. sunshine hen   hatmaker art   estimate _____

/ 7

15. apparent pan   outvoted toe   advocate _____
16. reappears pea   dividends din   modifiers _____
17. torturous out   epileptic pie   bloodshot _____
18. abundant and   sceptres set   handmaid _____
19. corroded rod   sweetens ewe   uprooted _____
20. waywardly way   weakening keg   dumbfound _____

/ 6

Complete a Word Pair

Find the word that completes the third pair of words so that it follows the same pattern as the first two pairs.

1.	anteater ate	flitting fit	journals _____
2.	safe pace	fork cook	yell _____
3.	contractor cot	heightened hen	kickstands _____
4.	slipperily lip	collection oil	distribute _____
5.	pinpoint nip	stiletto its	downcast _____
6.	giggling gig	fireside fir	habitual _____
7.	swallowable law	freehearted her	reinventing _____

/ 7

8.	dolloped old	priority rip	curtains _____
9.	taffeta fat	despite set	cohered _____
10.	amendment men	forewords ore	singularly _____
11.	joyously you	visitors sit	feasting _____
12.	barbarians bar	redressing red	indefinite _____
13.	waves raven	roped mopey	homey _____
14.	handshakes has	annoyingly any	originator _____
15.	embankment men	horsepower owe	clambering _____

/ 8

16.	gibbering big	mellowest let	triweekly _____
17.	flavourful flu	perpetuate pet	humidifier _____
18.	kookaburra oak	effervesce fee	friendlier _____
19.	undeluded due	abstracts sat	carefully _____
20.	annotation tan	ineptitude tie	auctioneer _____
21.	woodenware woe	applesauce ape	cartwheels _____
22.	appraisals spa	woodworker row	nationwide _____

/ 7

Closest Meaning

Underline two words, one from each set of brackets, that have the most similar meaning.

Look at this example:

(<u>reign</u>　throne　tyrant)　　　(dominion　<u>govern</u>　ruler)

1. (peek　squint　ogle)　　　(gape　blink　focus)

2. (saturated　moist　humid)　　　(parched　aquatic　sodden)

3. (revive　relinquish　redouble)　　　(remonstrate　resurrect　reward)

4. (custodian　governor　sentinel)　　　(delegate　magistrate　guard)

5. (asset　leverage　device)　　　(benefit　cache　stake)

6. (striking　promising　impending)　　　(upcoming　burgeoning　tantalising)

7. (overcome　command　trounce)　　　(vie　rout　excel)

/ 7

8. (flummox　exasperate　entice)　　　(bewilder　bequeath　besmirch)

9. (disclose　partake　annex)　　　(enlist　divulge　conserve)

10. (exemplary　requisite　practical)　　　(beneficial　specific　integral)

11. (eclipse　enhance　flourish)　　　(endure　surpass　exalt)

12. (award　furnish　donate)　　　(devote　peddle　equip)

13. (mortified　astounded　dismayed)　　　(enlivened　angered　flabbergasted)

14. (arresting　exacting　understanding)　　　(calculating　uplifting　demanding)

/ 7

15. (imprint　acronym　alias)　　　(signature　monogram　pseudonym)

16. (auxiliary　substandard　customary)　　　(respective　supplementary　unofficial)

17. (articulated　symbolic　implicit)　　　(obscure　momentous　unspoken)

18. (delicate　florid　luxurious)　　　(antique　ornate　priceless)

19. (esteemed　mediocre　negligible)　　　(adequate　minor　exclusive)

20. (dictionary　manual　compilation)　　　(appendix　anthology　record)

/ 6

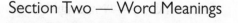

Closest Meaning

Underline two words, one from each set of brackets, that have the most similar meaning.

Hint: Cross out any words that you think are definitely wrong as you go along.

1. (fetid squalid murky)   (depraved filthy ruinous)

2. (affectionate obliging capable)   (accommodating candid generous)

3. (decimate pummel cleave)   (bludgeon ambush infiltrate)

4. (inhibit efface refine)   (erase review evaluate)

5. (bunker stronghold barrier)   (tower haven fortress)

6. (disconsolate vexed peevish)   (unkempt listless despondent)

7. (stigma bedlam quibble)   (objection remorse lamentation)

/ 7

8. (premature opportune idyllic)   (timely fortuitous prosperous)

9. (headstrong sprightly delightful)   (vivacious devout fanciful)

10. (hypocritical brazen vile)   (egotistical pretentious impertinent)

11. (straggler urchin scoundrel)   (oppressor outcast reprobate)

12. (fractious militant facetious)   (flippant divisive adamant)

13. (impactful fruitful arduous)   (poignant sensational tenacious)

14. (malevolent provocative sinister)   (crude impassioned inflammatory)

/ 7

15. (unfeeling petulant forlorn)   (clunky irascible mature)

16. (imperious august congenial)   (agreeable coordinated slick)

17. (recurrent changeable miraculous)   (mercurial temperate immoderate)

18. (tender resplendent decorous)   (lenient extravagant proper)

19. (principled prodigal thankless)   (provincial thriftless profane)

20. (pastoral urbane momentary)   (nomadic exotic bucolic)

/ 6

Section Two — Word Meanings

Opposite Meaning

Underline two words, one from each set of brackets, that have the most opposite meaning.

Look at this example:

(subtract   divide   <u>halve</u>)   (increase   <u>double</u>   twice)

1. (package   collapse   unfurl)   (segregate   fold   arrange)

2. (spindly   pallid   timid)   (stocky   lofty   mighty)

3. (comparable   phony   legitimate)   (unique   authentic   identical)

4. (shuffle   hurtle   meander)   (creep   cower   thrust)

5. (reckless   thoughtless   wasteful)   (frugal   mellow   sober)

6. (jubilant   optimistic   easygoing)   (luckless   ponderous   crestfallen)

7. (laud   spurn   provoke)   (distinguish   embrace   accentuate)

/ 7

8.   (leaden   jagged   rigid)   (compact   malleable   titanic)

9.   (dislodge   excavate   fuse)   (unearth   integrate   anchor)

10. (subdued   traitorous   irritable)   (distinctive   boisterous   personable)

11. (novelty   jeopardy   impunity)   (veracity   utility   security)

12. (prevalent   distinct   eccentric)   (uncommon   prominent   quaint)

13. (indulge   falter   daunt)   (incense   hearten   mystify)

14. (ludicrous   obscene   unorthodox)   (subjective   inoffensive   intimate)

/ 7

15. (gullible   assured   buoyant)   (insolent   insecure   untrained)

16. (ominous   inscrutable   erratic)   (encouraging   improbable   unforeseen)

17. (acuteness   proximity   density)   (estimation   scarcity   remoteness)

18. (festivity   positivity   cordiality)   (hostility   vulnerability   adversity)

19. (bemused   disgruntled   fazed)   (esteemed   infatuated   gratified)

20. (apprehend   abide   vent)   (circulate   repress   construe)

/ 6

Opposite Meaning

> Underline two words, one from each set of brackets, that have the most opposite meaning.

Hint: If you don't know the meaning of a word, try removing any prefixes and suffixes to see if you know the meaning of the root word.

1. (amass   exchange   relinquish)   (advertise   withhold   revere)
2. (obvious   calamitous   impulsive)   (calculated   inane   momentous)
3. (integrity   competence   solemnity)   (infirmity   indecision   deceitfulness)
4. (talentless   receptive   intuitive)   (accustomed   dedicated   learned)
5. (remiss   suboptimal   problematic)   (composed   unchecked   attentive)
6. (prudent   courteous   scrupulous)   (immoral   ravenous   radical)
7. (puncture   hollow   shaft)   (span   protrusion   sculpt)

/ 7

8. (deft   tactful   compliant)   (opinionated   servile   wayward)
9. (destitute   precarious   forlorn)   (covetous   opulent   enterprising)
10. (cultivate   liberate   authorise)   (subjugate   desecrate   dismantle)
11. (tacit   taboo   insincere)   (permissible   contentious   compelling)
12. (finicky   complimentary   adept)   (defamatory   partisan   contradictory)
13. (fortify   coalesce   displace)   (purge   preclude   debilitate)
14. (pragmatic   undisputed   aberrant)   (typical   contrary   complex)

/ 7

15. (mottled   incandescent   garish)   (dim   variegated   atmospheric)
16. (curtail   segment   expunge)   (regulate   intensify   preserve)
17. (convoluted   laborious   precarious)   (customary   direct   beneficial)
18. (fervent   meticulous   abstemious)   (cynical   unpretentious   gluttonous)
19. (imperious   belligerent   dynamic)   (peaceable   diplomatic   zealous)

/ 6

20. (loquacious   disarming   resolute)   (dispassionate   satirical   reticent)

Section Two — Word Meanings

Multiple Meanings

Choose the word that has a similar meaning to the words in both sets of brackets. Underline your answer.

Look at this example:

(cut reduce)	(jetty quay)	trim port prune <u>dock</u> crop

1. (key code)   (fable saga)   maxim cipher legend parable myth

2. (hex spell)   (swear blaspheme)   jinx profane curse charm conjuration

3. (pitch fling)   (initiate commence)   throw launch incite lob found

4. (twisted skewed)   (dishonest deceitful)   crooked gnarled tangled contorted twined

5. (tear rip)   (fragment smidgen)   sliver slit fray shred rupture

6. (bud origin)   (microbe bacterium)   root spore seed cell germ

/ 6

7. (brilliant great)   (implausible unreal)   excellent fantastic exotic splendid terrific

8. (jumble muddle)   (clamber climb)   scramble scale shuffle fluster mount

9. (detour deviation)   (amusement recreation)   leisure turn alteration circuit diversion

10. (closest adjacent)   (prompt instantaneous)   urgent nigh immediate pressing adjoining

11. (bug annoy)   (try attempt)   irk bother rile bid stab

12. (energetic lively)   (functional running)   alert active fluent on working

/ 6

13. (sharpen file)   (drudgery toil)   chore scour labour glaze grind

14. (tool utensil)   (execute effect)   agent implement device render action

15. (churn stir)   (upset perturb)   agitate disconcert ferment seethe spook

16. (hide skin)   (bombard hurl)   cast jacket sling pelt strike

17. (hitch pitfall)   (grab snatch)   pluck grasp snag glitch trap

18. (mend fix)   (condition state)   phase restore order repair doctor

/ 6

Multiple Meanings

> Choose the word that has a similar meaning to the words in both sets of brackets. Underline your answer.

1. (endure suffer)   (maintain preserve)   brave uphold sustain conserve weather

2. (affront slight)   (garble mumble)   slander stutter slur scorn stammer

3. (pause break)   (soothe settle)   lull lapse subdue respite hush

4. (frill ornament)   (pruning shearing)   paring trimming shaving snipping cutting

5. (squander waste)   (setback mishap)   upset hitch blow expend trifle

6. (bomb strike)   (husk casing)   shuck raid hull shell strafe

7. (barge pontoon)   (abundance profusion)   craft flood float glut raft

/ 7

8. (channel trench)   (pattern routine)   ditch paradigm trough order groove

9. (trace hint)   (misgiving distrust)   qualm suspicion hunch vestige remnant

10. (banish expel)   (disparage belittle)   deride oust decry dismiss dispel

11. (claim assertion)   (disagreement dispute)   clash contention allegation suit bout

12. (bang boom)   (account narrative)   tale crack report plot discharge

13. (rebuke castigate)   (explosion detonation)   clang blast burst beat slam

14. (coat fur)   (cheat defraud)   fleece pile wool down lint

/ 7

15. (caper frolic)   (search inspect)   gambol scour probe frisk cavort

16. (gush fawn)   (commotion furore)   squall rave fuss drool flap

17. (slay butcher)   (send convey)   desolate deliver dispatch delegate destroy

18. (assuage allay)   (replace supplant)   displace abate succeed mollify relieve

19. (lessen deplete)   (denigrate disparage)   asperse drain impugn diminish sap

20. (premium reward)   (generosity charity)   amity merit lenity bounty grant

/ 7

21. (broach raise)   (unresolved unsettled)   tender suspect moot open air

Odd Ones Out

Three of the words in each list are linked. Underline the two words that are not related to these three.

Look at this example:

archery   <u>skating</u>   <u>cycling</u>   darts   bowling

Hint: Check each answer by making sure you can explain exactly why the words are linked.

1. clip   badge   staple   pin   label

2. autobiography   newspaper   journal   magazine   thesaurus

3. projection   trend   forecast   assessment   estimation

4. stool   sofa   bench   couch   settee

5. allegory   folklore   fable   anecdote   parable

6. promote   incorporate   advocate   integrate   assimilate

/ 6

7. skirt   shroud   cloak   sleeve   mask

8. squelch   crunch   graze   collide   patter

9. hunch   inkling   premonition   conviction   wish

10. sled   cart   raft   trolley   wheelbarrow

11. dozen   batch   horde   multitude   swarm

12. forest   heath   canyon   moor   plain

/ 6

13. cavalry   armoury   artillery   ministry   infantry

14. frame   tapestry   engraving   canvas   mosaic

15. ingest   emit   discharge   exude   absorb

16. necklace   bracelet   locket   scarf   pendant

17. torrent   current   procession   flood   deluge

18. gland   pimple   rash   pustule   wart

/ 6

Section Two — Word Meanings

Odd Ones Out

Three of the words in each list are linked. Underline the two words that are not related to these three.

1. band   pair   unit   cluster   duo

2. redundant   excessive   sufficient   superfluous   inadequate

3. lawn   patio   veranda   conservatory   terrace

4. heroic   reckless   foolhardy   intrepid   madcap

5. indescribable   unutterable   unimaginable   unbelievable   inconceivable

6. spectral   spiritual   ghoulish   ethereal   ghostly

7. insignia   motif   hallmark   pattern   emblem

 / 7

8. escapism   evacuation   exclusion   exodus   emigration

9. gala   assembly   jamboree   conference   pageant

10. dialogue   sermon   soliloquy   monologue   discussion

11. pithy   succinct   witty   concise   apt

12. conscious   logical   mindful   ingenious   sentient

13. decanter   goblet   chalice   pitcher   tankard

14. tranquillity   gentility   propriety   politeness   serenity

 / 8

15. brick   clay   slate   peat   silt

16. critique   rant   review   tirade   diatribe

17. paradox   alliance   parallel   counterpart   equivalent

18. supervisor   magnate   mogul   merchant   tycoon

19. prudence   compassion   discretion   strategy   tact

20. sediment   dross   powder   scrap   chaff

21. bridge   piece   outro   track   chorus

 / 7

22. inherent   fledgling   incipient   budding   expiring

      Section Two — Word Meanings

Word Connections

> Choose two words, one from each set of brackets, that complete the sentence in the most sensible way. Underline both words.
>
> Look at this example:
>
> **Train** is to (track <u>station</u> wheel) as **plane** is to (gate fly <u>airport</u>).

1. **Century** is to (hundred decade history) as **millennium** is to (era modern thousand).

2. **Abundant** is to (hefty plentiful many) as **scarce** is to (scanty none select).

3. **Colander** is to (liquid holes strain) as **kettle** is to (electric water boil).

4. **Robust** is to (staunch flimsy sturdy) as **feeble** is to (old sluggish infirm).

5. **Assemble** is to (expand convene organise) as **disband** is to (disperse divide shrink).

6. **Sapling** is to (tree branch wood) as **bud** is to (shoot flower seed).

7. **Caravan** is to (trailer car mobile) as **plough** is to (farmer tractor field).

/ 7

8. **Impotent** is to (frenzied gallant powerful) as **inept** is to (accomplished wise useless).

9. **Offspring** is to (nature parents descendant) as **successor** is to (royalty estate heir).

10. **Deplore** is to (condemn approve repent) as **commend** is to (inflate reward laud).

11. **Fiasco** is to (success fail setback) as **feud** is to (squabble resolve bitterness).

12. **Thriller** is to (suspense film genre) as **comedy** is to (wit amusement farce).

13. **Iron** is to (steel forge metal) as **pottery** is to (knead kiln clay).

14. **Snake** is to (serpent reptile legs) as **human** is to (animal tail torso).

/ 7

15. **Arithmetic** is to (mathematics teach count) as **chemistry** is to (science learn reaction).

16. **Inspector** is to (constable police detective) as **admiral** is to (navy army ship).

17. **Uneasiness** is to (scare comfort phobia) as **fondness** is to (tender desire devotion).

18. **Employed** is to (salary occupation career) as **retired** is to (pension leisure elderly).

19. **Lanky** is to (tall gangly stumpy) as **scrawny** is to (stout slender attractive).

20. **Copper** is to (bronze mine rigid) as **oil** is to (well petrol fuel).

/ 6

Section Two — Word Meanings

Word Connections

Choose two words, one from each set of brackets, that complete the sentence in the most sensible way. Underline both words.

Hint: If you're stuck, try writing down how each word from the first set of brackets links to the word in bold. Then do the same for the second set of brackets and you should find a link that matches.

1. **Compensate** is to (money reimburse exchange) as **cheat** is to (dishonest swindle guile).

2. **Superficial** is to (cursory amiable profound) as **fickle** is to (varied genial faithful).

3. **Bulb** is to (electricity switch light) as **candle** is to (wick stick flame).

4. **Contentious** is to (fierce heated controversial) as **entrenched** is to (fluid forced established).

5. **Typewriter** is to (computer letters machine) as **sundial** is to (time shadows clock).

6. **Jittery** is to (blunt composed worry) as **testy** is to (cranky annoy easygoing).

7. **Hurricane** is to (tsunami cyclone wind) as **bog** is to (quagmire wet creek).

 / 7

8. **Trawler** is to (boat fishing voyage) as **crane** is to (lift machinery construction)

9. **Syringe** is to (water inject medicine) as **aerosol** is to (can spray graffiti).

10. **Society** is to (member club committee) as **trial** is to (participant science clinical).

11. **Jaded** is to (bejewelled drowsy invigorated) as **industrious** is to (bustling rural idle).

12. **Commandeer** is to (confiscate navigate forgo) as **waive** is to (gesture relinquish lose).

13. **Infringe** is to (tolerate scorn violate) as **obey** is to (provide conform defy).

14. **Crop** is to (harvest wheat food) as **timber** is to (forest log trees).

/ 7

15. **Uninspired** is to (riveting repetitive lacklustre) as **innovative** is to (creative precocious alert).

16. **Genealogy** is to (biology ancestry history) as **theology** is to (writing education religion).

17. **Bachelor** is to (marriage husband man) as **child** is to (teenager adulthood mother).

18. **District** is to (community city outskirts) as **country** is to (continent county border).

19. **Tax** is to (money government payment) as **rent** is to (landlord housing neighbour).

 / 6

20. **Alpine** is to (cold mountains land) as **maritime** is to (sea water ships).

Section Two — Word Meanings

Complete the Sum

Find the missing number to complete each sum.
Write your answer on the line.

Look at this example:

$$7 \times 3 - 5 + 9 = 5 \times (\underline{\;5\;})$$

1. $24 \div 3 + 12 - 8 = 4 \times (\underline{\quad})$

2. $6 \times 8 - 9 = 15 \div 5 \times (\underline{\quad})$

3. $7 \times 3 - 20 + 1 = (\underline{\quad}) \div 8$

4. $9 \times 7 - 14 + 3 = 13 \times (\underline{\quad})$

5. $35 \div 7 \times 9 - 18 = 3 \times (\underline{\quad})$

6. $56 \div 8 + 3 = 21 - (\underline{\quad}) + 1$

7. $6 \times 5 + 7 = (\underline{\quad}) \times 4 - 3$

> **Hint:** Don't use a calculator for these questions — you won't be allowed to use one in the test.

/ 7

8. $20 \div 4 \times 8 + 9 = (\underline{\quad}) \times 7$

9. $28 \div 4 \times 10 - 4 = 6 \times (\underline{\quad})$

10. $3 \times 12 \div 4 = 18 + 5 - (\underline{\quad})$

11. $45 \div 5 \times 7 + 9 = 8 \times (\underline{\quad})$

12. $12 \times 4 - 14 + 11 = 3 \times (\underline{\quad})$

13. $42 \div 7 + 17 = 6 \times 6 - (\underline{\quad})$

14. $18 \div 3 \times 11 + 18 = 12 \times (\underline{\quad})$

/ 7

15. $5 \times 12 \div 6 - 7 = (\underline{\quad}) \div 5$

16. $32 \div 8 \times 12 - 4 = 4 \times (\underline{\quad})$

17. $30 \div 6 + 18 = 41 - (\underline{\quad}) - 8$

18. $60 \div 4 + 14 = 43 - (\underline{\quad}) + 3$

19. $6 \times 5 + 11 - 9 = 41 - 13 + (\underline{\quad})$

20. $8 \times 3 - 7 + 15 = 6 \times (\underline{\quad}) - 10$

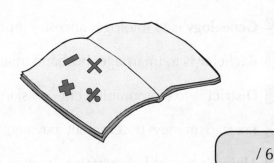

/ 6

Complete the Sum

Find the missing number to complete each sum.
Write your answer on the line.

1. $48 \div 12 + 7 - 5 = 3 \times 8 - (\underline{\quad})$

2. $6 \times 9 - 16 + 4 = 7 \times 5 + (\underline{\quad})$

3. $8 \times 5 \div 4 + 13 = 36 \div (\underline{\quad}) + 11$

4. $26 \div 2 - 7 + 21 = 6 \times 9 - (\underline{\quad})$

5. $11 \times 5 + 17 - 24 = (\underline{\quad}) - 14 + 29$

6. $5 \times 7 - 27 + 11 = 30 \div 5 + (\underline{\quad})$

7. $72 \div 6 - 9 + 18 = 7 \times 4 - (\underline{\quad})$

/ 7

8. $12 \times 4 - 16 + 29 = 9 \times 8 - (\underline{\quad})$

9. $81 \div 9 + 13 - 17 = (\underline{\quad}) \times 7 - 16$

10. $6 \times 6 \div 12 + 8 = 48 - (\underline{\quad}) + 23$

11. $88 \div 11 - 3 + 17 = 42 \div 6 + (\underline{\quad})$

12. $10 \times 9 + 23 - 75 = (\underline{\quad}) \times 6 - 22$

13. $12 \times 7 + 67 - 95 = 28 \div 4 \times (\underline{\quad})$

/ 7

14. $64 \div 8 \times 12 + 25 = 44 \div (\underline{\quad}) \times 11$

15. $11 \times 12 + 29 - 83 - 18 = 9 \times 4 + (\underline{\quad})$

16. $12 \times 10 \div 8 + 43 - 21 = 12 \times 5 - (\underline{\quad})$

17. $12 \times 7 \div 6 + 17 - 9 = 56 \div 8 + (\underline{\quad})$

18. $120 \div 12 \times 4 - 37 + 45 = (\underline{\quad}) \times 12 - 36$

19. $121 \div 11 \times 9 + 9 - 59 = 63 \div (\underline{\quad}) \times 7$

20. $9 \times 11 \div 3 + 18 - 23 = 12 \times 3 - (\underline{\quad})$

21. $72 \div 9 \times 12 - 19 - 38 = 21 \div (\underline{\quad}) \times 13$

/ 8

22. $144 \div 12 \times 11 - 37 - 19 = (\underline{\quad}) \times 8 - 20$

Letter Sequences

Find the pair of letters that continues each sequence in the best way. Use the alphabet to help you.

A B C D E F G H I J K L M N O P Q R S T U V W X Y Z

Look at this example:

| SU | QR | OO | ML | KI | (_IF_) |

1. FL   EN   CP   ZR   VT   (____)

2. ME   RI   UM   VQ   UU   (____)

3. SG   QJ   PN   NS   MY   (____)

4. RL   TI   VE   XZ   ZT   (____)

5. LJ   QK   UP   XQ   ZV   (____)

6. XR   WU   BZ   AG   FP   (____)

7. JQ   NS   TT   BV   LW   (____)

> **Hint:** The letters in a pair don't follow the same pattern, so make sure you check what each letter is doing.

/ 7

8. JG   NH   KK   OP   LW   (____)

9. SR   VN   QI   TC   OV   (____)

10. ZS   YN   VL   QG   JE   (____)

11. QG   SH   WL   CM   KQ   (____)

12. HP   DU   YY   UB   PD   (____)

13. NE   SB   PX   US   RM   (____)

14. UT   QU   PX   LC   KJ   (____)

/ 7

15. OM   RP   WR   ZS   ES   (____)

16. CW   AX   WA   QB   IE   (____)

17. TS   RT   WW   UB   ZI   (____)

18. LI   PG   VJ   DH   NK   (____)

19. QN   LP   FT   YV   QZ   (____)

20. NM   OI   OH   ND   LC   (____)

/ 6

Letter Sequences

Find the pair of letters that continues each sequence in the best way.
Use the alphabet to help you.

A B C D E F G H I J K L M N O P Q R S T U V W X Y Z

1. LG HJ GO CV BE (____)

2. QQ NM LJ IH GG (____)

3. AX EA KC SF CH (____)

4. DY AT ZM WD VS (____)

5. VF TD SA SY TV (____)

6. PK TH WD YA ZW (____)

7. BE WJ PH GM VK (____)

/ 7

8. DD AG ZK AN DR (____)

9. JI FL EQ AX ZG (____)

10. TC RZ OV MQ JK (____)

11. FH BM EP AQ DP (____)

12. QS MV GX YA OC (____)

13. GZ IV MP OH SX (____)

14. QQ TL OI RH MI (____)

/ 7

15. ZZ QP KX HB HD (____)

16. LE TZ QZ YE VO (____)

17. SP JT OB FN KD (____)

18. BM VB UI YX HE (____)

19. LW WT JV YR PO IQ (____)

20. AQ ES JQ DK HA MM (____)

21. FF KG RM GX LN SI (____)

22. CR KJ HE XC FD CH (____)

/ 8

Section Three — Maths and Sequences

Number Sequences

Find the number that continues each sequence in the best way.
Write your answer on the line.

Look at this example:

| 72 | 66 | 60 | 54 | 48 | (_42_) |

1. **4**   **9**   **13**   **22**   **35**   (____)

2. **64**   **63**   **60**   **55**   **48**   (____)

3. **5**   **7**   **10**   **15**   **22**   (____)

4. **3**   **28**   **6**   **14**   **12**   **7**   (____)

5. **77**   **52**   **36**   **27**   **23**   (____)

6. **5**   **53**   **77**   **89**   **95**   (____)

7. **1**   **3**   **2**   **6**   **4**   **12**   (____)

> **Hint:** Make sure you know sequences like prime and square numbers for the test.

/ 7

8. **2**   **19**   **34**   **47**   **58**   (____)

9. **45**   **41**   **35**   **27**   **17**   (____)

10. **64**   **59**   **52**   **41**   **28**   (____)

11. **14**   **19**   **33**   **52**   **85**   (____)

12. **200**   **136**   **104**   **88**   **80**   (____)

13. **2**   **1**   **8**   **4**   **32**   **16**   (____)

14. **7**   **32**   **48**   **57**   **61**   (____)

/ 7

15. **98**   **99**   **101**   **105**   **113**   (____)

16. **6**   **17**   **24**   **29**   **32**   (____)

17. **80**   **20**   **40**   **40**   **20**   **80**   (____)

18. **65**   **49**   **35**   **23**   **13**   (____)

19. **11**   **6**   **6**   **11**   **21**   (____)

20. **2**   **2**   **4**   **12**   (____)

/ 6

Number Sequences

Find the number that continues each sequence in the best way. Write your answer on the line.

1. 78   81   86   93   102   (____)

2. 50   39   32   27   24   (____)

3. 113   99   99   113   141   (____)

4. 1   1   3   12   9   23   (____)

5. 120   60   20   5   (____)

6. 55   54   50   41   25   (____)

7. 83   89   97   107   119   (____)

/ 7

8. 111   98   87   78   71   (____)

9. 3   7   16   32   57   (____)

10. 33   4   30   12   27   36   (____)

11. 3   15   60   180   (____)

12. 54   10   18   30   6   90   (____)

13. 40   32   32   8   24   2   (____)

14. 240   48   12   4   (____)

/ 7

15. 75   102   120   129   129   (____)

16. 4620   420   60   12   (____)

17. 3   12   4   6   7   2   (____)

18. 84   85   84   81   76   (____)

19. 945   105   15   3   1   (____)

20. 1   2   2   4   8   (____)

21. 1   8   27   64   (____)

22. 1   4   7   13   35   17   (____)

/ 8

Section Three — Maths and Sequences

Related Numbers

Find the number that completes the final set of numbers in the same way as the first two sets. Write your answer on the line.

Look at this example:

> 2 (5) 3   4 (9) 5   8 (_18_) 10

1. 4 (18) 5   3 (26) 10   5 (____) 7

2. 10 (6) 3   10 (20) 10   1 (____) 5

3. 4 (18) 2   8 (33) 3   5 (____) 4

4. 9 (9) 45   2 (11) 14   12 (____) 36

5. 11 (1) 6   17 (13) 15   7 (____) 11

6. 8 (3) 17   1 (8) 25   2 (____) 23

7. 4 (12) 9   6 (14) 7   6 (____) 9

/ 7

8. 24 (16) 3   21 (6) 7   48 (____) 8

9. 1 (5) 14   10 (4) 2   3 (____) 6

10. 2 (6) 7   9 (4) 31   7 (____) 37

11. 9 (17) 72   12 (17) 60   8 (____) 64

12. 6 (64) 2   2 (100) 8   3 (____) 2

13. 9 (7) 18   2 (11) 12   4 (____) 20

14. 21 (26) 29   13 (19) 23   12 (____) 22

/ 7

15. 4 (19) 3   6 (34) 6   1 (____) 10

16. 7 (25) 7   3 (8) 5   9 (____) 3

17. 8 (16) 14   2 (14) 16   10 (____) 12

18. 2 (5) 10   13 (8) 27   17 (____) 33

19. 4 (33) 18   3 (18) 9   2 (____) 6

20. 28 (13) 7   15 (10) 3   36 (____) 6

Hint: Some of the trickier questions require a calculation with up to three steps.

/ 6

Section Three — Maths and Sequences

Related Numbers

Find the number that completes the final set of numbers in the same way as the first two sets. Write your answer on the line.

1. 70 (50) 24   23 (23) 17   14 (____) 18

2. 5 (14) 4   11 (48) 8   6 (____) 9

3. 10 (49) 2   8 (28) 4   21 (____) 3

4. 19 (34) 8   14 (37) 2   16 (____) 9

5. 3 (40) 7   5 (56) 9   6 (____) 10

6. 7 (24) 49   2 (39) 24   5 (____) 55

7. 15 (39) 2   12 (21) 5   20 (____) 4

/ 7

8. 1 (12) 15   6 (22) 20   5 (____) 15

9. 6 (7) 3   5 (8) 4   13 (____) 4

10. 4 (23) 8   2 (29) 26   1 (____) 13

11. 5 (3) 9   13 (4) 19   37 (____) 71

12. 3 (9) 9   1 (36) 6   2 (____) 8

13. 30 (25) 9   14 (12) 4   16 (____) 1

14. 3 (5) 9   2 (7) 8   1 (____) 10

/ 7

15. 3 (19) 5   2 (23) 10   7 (____) 9

16. 1 (36) 5   2 (25) 3   5 (____) 3

17. 4 (18) 8   3 (9) 5   4 (____) 6

18. 6 (4) 12   1 (5) 9   7 (____) 9

19. 2 (10) 4   5 (13) 1   3 (____) 7

20. 2 (22) 5   4 (98) 6   3 (____) 8

21. 16 (18) 5   8 (10) 3   14 (____) 2

22. 5 (31) 4   4 (16) 3   8 (____) 2

/ 8

Letter-Coded Sums

Each letter stands for a number. Work out the answer to each sum as a letter. Write your answer on the line.

Look at this example:

A = 2   B = 4   C = 5   D = 7   E = 10   A + C + D − E = (__B__)

1.   A = 6   B = 11   C = 17   D = 22   E = 23   A + E + B − C = (____)

2.   A = 5   B = 6   C = 8   D = 10   E = 34   C × B − E − C = (____)

3.   A = 4   B = 5   C = 12   D = 27   E = 28   C × B − D − B = (____)

4.   A = 11   B = 16   C = 19   D = 25   E = 38   E ÷ C + D − B = (____)

5.   A = 9   B = 10   C = 21   D = 22   E = 44   E ÷ D + A + B = (____)

/ 5

6.   A = 7   B = 9   C = 11   D = 25   E = 28   E ÷ A × B − C = (____)

7.   A = 12   B = 19   C = 22   D = 36   E = 38   D ÷ A + E − C = (____)

8.   A = 7   B = 8   C = 22   D = 24   E = 26   D ÷ B + E − A = (____)

9.   A = 2   B = 12   C = 36   D = 28   E = 40   E × A − D − B = (____)

10. A = 5   B = 9   C = 27   D = 32   E = 36   E ÷ B + D − C = (____)

/ 5

11. A = 9   B = 15   C = 18   D = 24   E = 39   C ÷ A × B + A = (____)

12. A = 11   B = 18   C = 26   D = 33   E = 40   D ÷ A + C − A = (____)

13. A = 7   B = 12   C = 17   D = 25   E = 28   E ÷ A + D − B = (____)

14. A = 5   B = 6   C = 9   D = 12   E = 13   B × D ÷ C + A = (____)

15. A = 8   B = 12   C = 28   D = 43   E = 45   B × A − E − D = (____)

/ 6

16. A = 6   B = 12   C = 16   D = 24   E = 32   C × A ÷ B + D = (____)

Section Three — Maths and Sequences

Letter-Coded Sums

Each letter stands for a number. Work out the answer to each sum as a letter. Write your answer on the line.

1. A = 3   B = 7   C = 15   D = 16   E = 27   E ÷ A + D − B − A = (_____)

2. A = 4   B = 8   C = 10   D = 23   E = 26   C × A ÷ B + E − D = (_____)

3. A = 6   B = 8   C = 15   D = 18   E = 22   D ÷ A + E − C + B = (_____)

4. A = 9   B = 11   C = 13   D = 22   E = 29   D ÷ B + E − C − A = (_____)

5. A = 7   B = 9   C = 17   D = 25   E = 28   E ÷ A × B + C − E = (_____)

6. A = 4   B = 8   C = 12   D = 20   E = 32   B ÷ A × C + D − C = (_____)

/ 6

7. A = 4   B = 8   C = 9   D = 16   E = 28   D ÷ A × C − D + B = (_____)

8. A = 3   B = 6   C = 11   D = 14   E = 18   C × B ÷ A + D − E = (_____)

9. A = 5   B = 10   C = 15   D = 22   E = 25   C ÷ A + D − A − B = (_____)

10. A = 4   B = 9   C = 12   D = 24   E = 45   E ÷ B × C ÷ A + B = (_____)

11. A = 5   B = 9   C = 29   D = 32   E = 50   E ÷ A × B − C − D = (_____)

12. A = 5   B = 7   C = 13   D = 30   E = 33   C × A − D + A − E = (_____)

/ 6

13. A = 11   B = 13   C = 44   D = 59   E = 60   A × B − D − E − A = (_____)

14. A = 4   B = 8   C = 10   D = 12   E = 16   B × D ÷ E × A − D − B = (_____)

15. A = 2   B = 3   C = 5   D = 12   E = 15   D ÷ A × B × C ÷ E − B = (_____)

16. A = 6   B = 8   C = 9   D = 16   E = 21   A × B ÷ D × E ÷ C + C = (_____)

17. A = 6   B = 10   C = 12   D = 18   E = 66   E ÷ A × C ÷ A − D + A = (_____)

18. A = 3   B = 9   C = 36   D = 63   E = 81   C × A ÷ B + E − D + A + A = (_____)

/ 6

Letter Connections

Mark the pair of letters that completes each sentence in the most sensible way. Use the alphabet to help you.

A B C D E F G H I J K L M N O P Q R S T U V W X Y Z

Look at this example:

CA is to **FD** as **KI** is to (IG   PN   <u>NL</u>   OM   ML).

1. **UN** is to **QH** as **TR** is to   (OM   PM   PL   NL   LP).

2. **GQ** is to **NT** as **BC** is to   (IF   HE   HF   IG   JE).

3. **CW** is to **XO** as **JB** is to   (DT   DQ   FS   ER   ET).

4. **KV** is to **EP** as **IC** is to   (XS   XR   SY   RX   QY).

5. **WF** is to **DA** as **LB** is to   (RW   RV   UX   SW   SV).

6. **HS** is to **JQ** as **BY** is to   (DW   TG   CX   GT   WD).

7. **XY** is to **OP** as **CD** is to   (UV   RT   TV   TU   ST).

/ 7

8. **EY** is to **WE** as **VZ** is to   (MF   NE   MD   NF   OE).

9. **UA** is to **AT** as **GV** is to   (NO   MO   MP   NP   PM).

10. **AZ** is to **FU** as **GT** is to   (LO   NO   KP   LN   LM).

11. **NM** is to **IR** as **JQ** is to   (KP   EV   BY   DW   CX).

12. **TU** is to **AP** as **WZ** is to   (EU   DW   FU   ET   DU).

13. **JX** is to **BB** as **SK** is to   (KG   AO   KO   AP   LN).

14. **DQ** is to **JW** as **UN** is to   (AZ   MF   ZA   FM   TG).

/ 7

15. **BY** is to **VE** as **FU** is to   (ZA   BY   YB   AZ   GT).

16. **FI** is to **OY** as **QD** is to   (YS   ZX   AU   ZT   AT).

17. **OL** is to **KQ** as **GT** is to   (BY   DX   CY   DZ   BX).

18. **GT** is to **KP** as **IR** is to   (MN   UF   OL   EV   DW).

19. **BA** is to **MC** as **YI** is to   (IK   JK   KJ   LM   IM).

20. **LO** is to **SH** as **YB** is to   (PK   NM   EV   CX   FU).

/ 6

  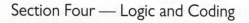

Letter Connections

Mark the pair of letters that completes each sentence in the most sensible way. Use the alphabet to help you.

A B C D E F G H I J K L M N O P Q R S T U V W X Y Z

1. **TA** is to **HW** as **DD** is to (RZ   SY   RY   SA   RA).

2. **JH** is to **SQ** as **CZ** is to (YA   BX   XA   AX   YB).

3. **NU** is to **UI** as **DJ** is to (JY   KX   JX   LW   NZ).

4. **PB** is to **GL** as **UV** is to (LE   KF   KD   ME   LF).

5. **DD** is to **VR** as **PT** is to (FG   GH   II   HH   IJ).

6. **BY** is to **RI** as **GT** is to (OL   HS   EV   WD   PK).

7. **ZA** is to **UF** as **WD** is to (SH   RI   NM   TG   SJ).

/ 7

8. **AF** is to **UY** as **PU** is to (JN   KM   KN   OL   JM).

9. **OY** is to **GE** as **HI** is to (AK   BL   ZO   ZM   AL).

10. **MX** is to **RF** as **TW** is to (ZB   YF   YE   AD   XC).

11. **NV** is to **EM** as **YP** is to (PY   KB   OL   BK   LO).

12. **KP** is to **QJ** as **CX** is to (JQ   BY   EV   IR   FU).

13. **CD** is to **LY** as **IP** is to (RM   TK   PK   SL   RK).

14. **UF** is to **BY** as **DW** is to (NM   GT   QJ   KP   LO).

/ 7

15. **ZA** is to **SH** as **CX** is to (UF   VE   RI   TG   QJ).

16. **BO** is to **UU** as **LL** is to (RR   FQ   ER   DS   SD).

17. **JM** is to **QN** as **FU** is to (MV   LW   LU   NW   MU).

18. **DP** is to **PC** as **IX** is to (UJ   UK   TK   UL   VK).

19. **GJ** is to **QZ** as **BA** is to (MS   OR   LQ   OP   NQ).

20. **KJ** is to **YR** as **EN** is to (TV   TU   SV   SU   RV).

21. **YB** is to **MM** as **CC** is to (IN   QM   QI   QN   PN).

22. **VE** is to **MN** as **SH** is to (OL   JQ   IR   EV   FU).

/ 8

Letter-Word Codes

Each question uses a different code. Use the alphabet to help you work out the answer to each question.

A B C D E F G H I J K L M N O P Q R S T U V W X Y Z

Look at this example:

If the code for **BOX** is **CPY**, what is the code for **HIT**? _____ IJU _____

1. If the code for **LIVE** is **NKXG**, what is the code for **GOLD**? _____

2. If the code for **HELM** is **EBIJ**, what is **HFKA** the code for? _____

3. If the code for **RUST** is **NQOP**, what is the code for **SLIP**? _____

4. If the code for **SALT** is **HZOG**, what is **XIVD** the code for? _____

5. If the code for **BLOW** is **ZNMY**, what is the code for **TIME**? _____

/ 5

6. If the code for **RAIN** is **PEGR**, what is the code for **ZERO**? _____

7. If the code for **TWO** is **SUL**, what is **GCO** the code for? _____

8. If the code for **HOPE** is **SLKV**, what is **IZMG** the code for? _____

9. If the code for **DREAM** is **HOIXQ**, what is the code for **SWIFT**? _____

10. If the code for **CLASP** is **DNDWU**, what is **ZWPQD** the code for? _____

/ 5

11. If the code for **ANGRY** is **DPHRX**, what is **ENVSG** the code for? _____

12. If the code for **LATER** is **QXYBW**, what is the code for **TOUGH**? _____

13. If the code for **STUNG** is **QYSSE**, what is the code for **FLAKE**? _____

14. If the code for **QUILT** is **RWLPY**, what is **DJHWY** the code for? _____

15. If the code for **PORCH** is **KLIXS**, what is **HORNV** the code for? _____

/ 5

Letter-Word Codes

Each question uses a different code. Use the alphabet to help you work out the answer to each question.

A B C D E F G H I J K L M N O P Q R S T U V W X Y Z

1. If the code for **INBOX** is **JKCLY**, what is the code for **POWER**? _____

2. If the code for **JOKED** is **ESFIY**, what is the code for **SLANT**? _____

3. If the code for **GUARD** is **EQUNB**, what is **NKOYF** the code for? _____

4. If the code for **ORDER** is **LWAJO**, what is the code for **FIGHT**? _____

5. If the code for **HOME** is **EKJA**, what is **DHXZ** the code for? _____

6. If the code for **LIGHT** is **NEIDV**, what is **DHCJM** the code for? _____

/ 6

7. If the code for **HAUNT** is **SZFMG**, what is the code for **NOVEL**? _____

8. If the code for **THUMB** is **VIULZ**, what is **HMARF** the code for? _____

9. If the code for **MUNCH** is **MSJWZ**, what is the code for **DRINK**? _____

10. If the code for **FACES** is **HEIMC**, what is **FEOAI** the code for? _____

11. If the code for **UNIT** is **SSGY**, what is **KTPJ** the code for? _____

12. If the code for **STAIN** is **NQZJQ**, what is the code for **FLUTE**? _____

/ 6

13. If the code for **PEARL** is **MHYTK**, what is the code for **YACHT**? _____

14. If the code for **RADIO** is **SYGET**, what is **TRBHJ** the code for? _____

15. If the code for **ACTIVE** is **ZETHXE**, what is the code for **MONTHS**? _____

16. If the code for **VOICE** is **VQEIW**, what is **CJWUK** the code for? _____

17. If the code for **FABRIC** is **HZBTHC**, what is the code for **PONDER**? _____

18. If the code for **ZEBRA** is **ABGKJ**, what is **MXULN** the code for? _____

19. If the code for **YELLOW** is **WGIOKA**, what is the code for **SPRING**? _____

/ 7

Section Four — Logic and Coding

Number-Word Codes

The number codes for three of these four words are listed in a random order. Work out the code to answer the questions.

VOLE   **WOVE**   **EVIL**   **VIEW**

2316   4532   3124

1.   Find the code for the word **WOVE**.   _____

2.   Find the code for the word **VEIL**.   _____

3.   Find the word that has the number code **6532**.   _____

/ 3

CAME   **RACE**   **MORE**   **CRAM**

5416   1436   3256

4.   Find the code for the word **RACE**.   _____

5.   Find the code for the word **ORCA**.   _____

6.   Find the word that has the number code **3456**.   _____

/ 3

ETCH   **FETA**   **CHEF**   **FACT**

3264   6431   1325

7.   Find the code for the word **FACT**.   _____

8.   Find the code for the word **CAFE**.   _____

9.   Find the word that has the number code **4312**.   _____

/ 3

SLOT   **ROSE**   **LOST**   **SORE**

4132   3412   5136

10. Find the code for the word **SORE**.   _____

11. Find the code for the word **TOES**.   _____

12. Find the word that has the number code **5632**.   _____

/ 3

Section Four — Logic and Coding

Number-Word Codes

> The number codes for three of these four words are listed in a random order. Work out the code to answer the questions.

TRIM   UNIT   RUIN   RUNT

1645   2341   6243

1. Find the code for the word **UNIT**. _____

2. Find the code for the word **TURN**. _____

3. Find the word that has the number code **5431**. _____

/ 3

GLAD   CLOG   CLAD   GOAL

6531   1325   1524

4. Find the code for the word **CLAD**. _____

5. Find the code for the word **GOLD**. _____

6. Find the word that has the number code **5324**. _____

/ 3

EASY   POLE   SALE   POSY

4123   6754   2154

7. Find the code for the word **POLE**. _____

8. Find the code for the word **SLAY**. _____

9. Find the word that has the number code **7615**. _____

/ 3

GRAM   FARE   FARM   BRAG

7241   5423   3426

10. Find the code for the word **FARM**. _____

11. Find the code for the word **MEGA**. _____

12. Find the word that has the number code **5124**. _____

/ 3

Explore the Facts

Read the information carefully, then use it to answer the question that follows. Write your answer on the line.

1. Mel, Jake, Kwame, Sally and Bitna go to an ice-cream parlour.

   Mel, Jake and Sally all get sprinkles on their ice-cream. Bitna gets three toppings. Everyone gets chocolate sauce except Kwame. Bitna, Jake, Sally and Mel all get raspberries. Kwame and Jake both get chopped nuts. Bitna is the only one to get a cherry.

   Who has the **most** toppings? _____   / 1

2. Valeria, Louis, Chantel, Samuel and Rachel are drawing pictures of their favourite vegetables.

   Samuel and Louis both draw carrots and parsnips. No one except Chantel draws beans. Everyone draws cabbages except Louis. Chantel and Louis draw turnips. Rachel is the only one to draw radishes. Samuel, Valeria and Rachel all draw cabbages and onions.

   Who draws the **fewest** vegetables? _____   / 1

3. Molly, Benji, Toby, Amna and Ferne compete in events at an athletics competition.

   Everyone except Amna competes in the hammer throw, javelin throw and shot put. Amna and Benji both compete in the 100 m sprint and the triple jump. Molly and Ferne are the only ones to take part in the high jump and discus. Toby competes in the pole vault, shot put and long jump. Benji withdraws from the hurdles, but Amna and Ferne still compete.

   Who competes in the **most** events? _____   / 1

4. Megan, Dan, Sakura, Robbie and Nick all collect items on a nature walk.

   Dan, Sakura and Robbie all collect pinecones and wildflowers. Four of the children collect sticks. Megan collects four different items. Nick is the only one to collect conkers and stones. Sakura, Robbie and Megan all collect leaves. Dan does not collect sticks. Robbie is the only one to collect acorns.

   Who collects the **most** items? _____   / 1

Explore the Facts

Read the information carefully, then use it to answer the question that follows. Write your answer on the line.

Hint: For trickier questions, it can help to draw a table with all the information in it.

1. Tim, Kia, Dax, Zuri and Jakub are discussing their favourite breakfasts.

    Three people like cereal. Kia, Jakub and Zuri like porridge. As well as eggs, the only types of breakfast Tim likes are pancakes, fruit or toast. Kia likes three types of breakfast. Dax likes pancakes, eggs and fruit, but he doesn't like cereal. Everyone likes eggs except Kia. Dax and Jakub like porridge and toast. Zuri's favourite breakfast is fruit.

    Who likes the **fewest** types of breakfast food? _____

    / 1

2. Lily, Jaxon, Skye, Fiona and Pav all order toasties for lunch.

    There are six toastie toppings available. Four people order cheese. Jaxon and Pav order ham, cheese and tomato toasties. Skye and Lily both ask for onion and red pepper. Skye orders more than half the toppings available. No one orders tuna except Fiona. Lily orders ham but no cheese in her toastie. Pav and Fiona order tomato.

    Who has the **most** ingredients in their toastie? _____

    / 1

3. Hamza, Beth, Mason, Lauren and Ace are browsing books in the library.

    Beth and Mason both read three pages of 'Space Secrets'. Ace reads five pages of 'Pirate Plot'. Ace chooses to read a page of 'Circus Mania' instead of 'Dragon Diaries'. Hamza, Beth and Lauren all read four pages of 'Sunshine in Paris'. Mason reads three pages each of 'Pirate Plot' and 'Space Secrets'. Hamza decides against reading 'Dragon Diaries', but three of the other children read a page. Everyone but Lauren reads the first page of 'Circus Mania'.

    Who reads the **most** pages? _____

    / 1

4. Eden, Rhea, Charlie, Tom and Abeni are talking about the meals they ate at school last week.

    The school canteen serves one hot meal a day, but children can bring a packed lunch instead. Two of the children had chicken pie. Three of the children had veggie curry on Thursday, and everyone except Charlie had cheese pasta on Tuesday. Abeni ate all the hot meals, except the ones that contained meat. Tom and Charlie are the only ones who had beef burgers on Friday and the only ones who didn't have lentil soup. Tom only brought in a packed lunch on Monday and Wednesday. Eden ate three hot meals, including veggie curry.

    Who ate the **fewest** hot meals last week? _____

    / 1

Solve the Riddle

Read the information carefully, then use it to answer the question that follows. Underline the correct answer.

1. Kelly, Fran, Sanjay, Will and Patience all queue outside a shop to buy limited edition trainers. The shop opened at 9 am. Sanjay arrived 15 minutes after Kelly. Patience was not the last person to arrive. Fran joined the queue half an hour before Sanjay and she was the first in line. Kelly arrived an hour before the shop opened. Will arrived 10 minutes before the shop opened.

   If these statements are true, only one of the sentences below **must** be true. Which one?

   A Sanjay arrived before Patience.

   B Will arrived before Kelly.

   C Fran arrived at 7.40.

   D Patience arrived between 7.45 and 8.50.

   E Will was the fourth person to arrive.

2. Jordan, Seb, Olivia, Lucy and Saleem are playing with some marbles. There are red, blue and yellow marbles. Each child has three marbles. Seb has two blue marbles and one yellow marble. Jordan has three red marbles. Olivia and Saleem both have one yellow marble. Lucy has the same colour marbles as Seb. The most common colour is red.

   If these statements are true, only one of the sentences below **cannot** be true. Which one?

   A Only one person has three different colours.

   B There are five blue marbles in total.

   C Jordan is the only child without a blue marble.

   D Three people have red marbles.

   E Saleem has two blue marbles.

3. Kaya, Harley, Nathan, Max and Jade time how long they can hold their breath underwater. Max held his breath for 8.6 seconds. Kaya held her breath for half as long as Harley. The longest breath hold was 3.2 seconds longer than the second longest breath hold. Harley held his breath for 6.2 seconds. The shortest breath hold was 3.1 seconds.

   If these statements are true, only one of the sentences below **cannot** be true. Which one?

   A The longest breath hold was 11.8 seconds.

   B Kaya held her breath for the shortest time.

   C Harley held his breath for the second longest length of time.

   D Jade held her breath for 6.4 seconds.

   E Nathan held his breath longest.

 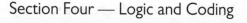

Solve the Riddle

Read the information carefully, then use it to answer the question that follows. Underline the correct answer.

1. Matthew, Niamh, Bea, Cillian and Rhys all get on the school bus at different times.
    Bea gets on at 8.02. Rhys and Cillian have the longest gap between them being
    picked up by the bus. Matthew is the second to get on the bus. Niamh gets on
    the bus 20 minutes after Cillian gets on. Matthew gets on 12 minutes before Bea.

    If these statements are true, only one of the sentences below **must** be true. Which one?

    A Bea gets on the bus second last.

    B Rhys gets on the bus at 8.10.

    C Matthew gets on the bus after Niamh.

    D Bea gets on the bus before Niamh.

    E Cillian gets on the bus after 7.30.

     / 1

2. Meredith, Ollie, Charlotte, Finn and Surya are competing in a climbing competition.
    There are 10 climbing walls and they get 10 points for each one they get to the top of.
    They get five points if they only reach halfway. Finn missed out on winning by 10
    points. Everyone got to the top of at least 3 walls, but no one got to the top of more than
    7. Ollie got halfway up 6 walls, which was the most points anyone else got for getting
    halfway. The winner had a score of 85. Meredith and Charlotte both got 50 points.

    If these statements are true, only one of the sentences below **must** be true. Which one?

    A Ollie came third.

    B Ollie scored 60 points.

    C Meredith got to the top of 5 walls.

    D Charlotte got halfway up 2 walls.

    E Surya got to the top of more walls than anyone else.

     / 1

3. Verity, Callum, Haitao, Keisha and Jessica are on a bike ride.
    Keisha cycled 4 km further than Haitao. Verity was the only person who
    cycled less than 10 km. The furthest distance cycled was 22 km. Haitao
    cycled twice as far as Verity. Verity and Jessica's combined distance was
    6 km further than the furthest distance. Callum cycled the second furthest.

    If these statements are true, only one of the sentences below **must** be true. Which one?

    A Callum cycled further than Jessica.

    B Haitao cycled the second shortest distance.

    C Callum cycled 20 km.

    D Jessica cycled the furthest.

    E Keisha cycled 14 km further than Verity.

 / 1

Section Four — Logic and Coding

Assessment Test 1

The rest of this book contains three assessment tests, which get progressively harder.

Allow 60 minutes to do each test and work as quickly and as carefully as you can.

If you want to attempt each test more than once, you will need to print **multiple-choice answer sheets** for these questions from our website — go to cgpbooks.co.uk/11plus/answer-sheets or scan the QR code on the right. If you'd prefer to answer the questions on the page, just follow the instructions in the question.

Answer Sheets

The number codes for three of these four words are listed in a random order. Work out the code to answer the questions.

RIOT   TOUR   TRIP   POUT

5364   2614   4532

1. Find the code for the word **TOUR**.   (_____)

2. Find the code for the word **PORT**.   (_____)

3. Find the word that has the number code **4536**.   (_____)

/ 3

The number codes for three of these four words are listed in a random order. Work out the code to answer the questions.

BAKE   SEAL   SLAB   BASK

3154   2561   3452

4. Find the code for the word **BASK**.   (_____)

5. Find the code for the word **ELKS**.   (_____)

6. Find the word that has the number code **6541**.   (_____)

/ 3

Mark two words, one from each set of brackets, that have the most similar meaning.

Example: (excited hopeful <u>sad</u>)   (angry <u>unhappy</u> lucky)

7. (demand challenge question)   (pressure insist claim)

8. (mistake doubt dilemma)   (quandary accident conflict)

9. (transient prompt fading)   (abrupt fleeting unwavering)

10. (deplorable trite mundane)   (substandard unoriginal ambitious)

11. (advocate prefer glorify)   (support ratify accredit)

/ 5

Mark the pair of letters that completes each sentence in the most sensible way. Use the alphabet to help you.

A B C D E F G H I J K L M N O P Q R S T U V W X Y Z

Example: DK is to **FM** as **PT** is to   (RS   <u>RV</u>   QV   QW   RU).

12.   **HS** is to **LO** as **BY** is to   (DW   EV   FU   CX   GT).

13.   **GO** is to **CU** as **KX** is to   (GC   HB   ID   GD   HF).

14.   **VB** is to **DS** as **NA** is to   (VR   VS   UW   WT   WR).

15.   **QT** is to **JZ** as **OM** is to   (GU   IS   GT   HS   HU).

16.   **WP** is to **KD** as **EI** is to   (RU   RV   UR   US   VR).

/ 5

Mark a word from the first set, followed by a word from the second set, that go together to form a new word.

Example: (<u>sun</u> shine hot)   (tree <u>flower</u> grass)   (the new word is 'sunflower')

17. (fast driver mile)   (way age ten)

18. (graves birth live)   (hood stone yard)

19. (fore inter front)   (tier sight rim)

20. (more panic neck)   (king tar bid)

21. (decade flip ramp)   (dent pant page)

22. (mute rival serve)   (vice ant led)

23. (count car heart)   (apart ten nation)

/ 7

Three of the words in each list are linked. Mark the two words that are not related to these three.

Example: jump   hop   <u>stroll</u>   leap   <u>hike</u>

24. pharmacy   cinema   bank   park   gym

25. fortify   buttress   construct   overhaul   strengthen

26. turmeric   salt   nutmeg   salsa   saffron

27. cover   hip   spine   shield   page

28. through   over   though   across   afterwards

/ 5

Carry on to the next question → →

Assessment Test 1

29. Polly, Luke, Britney, Francesco and Yael have all visited different cities.

   Britney and Luke have been to Edinburgh and Newcastle. Luke has also been to Brighton.
   Yael has visited Leicester, which Polly has too, but only Polly and Francesco have visited York.
   No one but Francesco has been to Cardiff, and only Britney has visited Manchester.
   Everyone but Yael has been to Brighton. Francesco, Luke and Yael have been to Edinburgh
   and Oxford together, and Luke went to Newcastle on his way to Edinburgh.

   Who has visited the **most** cities?   (_____)

30. Arthur, Oliver, Salma, Chloe and Julek all went rockpooling.

   Julek and Oliver both found two hermit crabs. Salma found five sea anemones but no starfish, and
   she found two sea snails, which was half the sea snails that Chloe found. Arthur, Julek and Chloe all
   found three mussels, and Oliver found two shore crabs to add to his two hermit crabs. Julek didn't
   find any starfish, but three children found one. Four children found only two sea snails each.

   Who found the **most** sea creatures?   (_____)   / 2

31. **Random** is to (confused arbitrary aimless) as **deliberate** is to (voluntary studied rash).

32. **Implausible** is to (viable exact questionable) as **copious** is to (cramped sparse miniature).

33. **Printer** is to (scan computer ink) as **car** is to (wheel petrol mirror).

34. **Distant** is to (aloof callous diffident) as **friendly** is to (affable indulgent devoted).

35. **Boxing** is to (gloves match ring) as **cricket** is to (catch field bowler).   / 5

36. year (grey) ogre   eras (_____) race

37. goes (some) smog   star (_____) atop

38. slit (list) stew   spam (_____) limp

39. snub (burn) curb   arts (_____) grit

40. ripe (pipe) epic   arid (_____) crag   / 5

Assessment Test 1

Find the letter that will finish the first word and start the second word of each pair. The same letter must be used for both pairs. **Either** mark the letter on the answer sheet, **or** write it on the line.

Example: cam (?) alm   bli (?) ole   (___p___)

41. dis (?) alf   chi (?) url   (_____)

42. ta (?) eep   hel (?) aft   (_____)

43. lea (?) ace   sel (?) ont   (_____)

44. sho (?) age   fla (?) ake   (_____)

45. wee (?) ing   bea (?) eel   (_____)

/ 5

Mark two words, one from each set of brackets, that have the most opposite meaning.

Example: (<u>wide</u> large high)   (long <u>narrow</u> short)

46. (credible eminent viable)   (fabricated untrustworthy dishonourable)

47. (hearten console pacify)   (impel hesitate provoke)

48. (establish vindicate affirm)   (disprove vanish neglect)

49. (unassuming meek forbearing)   (conceited spoilt callous)

50. (indignant notorious forlorn)   (prosperous illustrious impressive)

/ 5

Each letter stands for a number. Work out the answer to each sum as a letter.

Example: A = 3 B = 6 C = 7 D = 10 E = 12   A + D − C = (__B__)

51. A = 6 B = 9 C = 15 D = 18 E = 21   B × A − C − D = (_____)

52. A = 3 B = 8 C = 12 D = 18 E = 24   E ÷ B + C − A = (_____)

53. A = 4 B = 8 C = 12 D = 19 E = 25   A × B − E + C = (_____)

54. A = 5 B = 7 C = 11 D = 25 E = 30   D ÷ A × B − E = (_____)

55. A = 7 B = 9 C = 16 D = 18 E = 21   E ÷ A × B − D = (_____)

56. A = 5 B = 9 C = 12 D = 16 E = 22   A × C − E − D = (_____)

/ 6

Carry on to the next question → →

Assessment Test 1

In each sentence below a four-letter word is hidden at the end of one word and the start of the next. **Either** mark the part of the sentence that contains the hidden word on the answer sheet, **or** write the hidden word on the line.

Example: I get a heada<u>che at</u> night.   (<u>heat</u>)

57. Our new patio area seems popular.   (_____)

58. Their choir only sing contemporary music.   (_____)

59. We exercise together once a week.   (_____)

60. They teach many able students there.   (_____)

61. His orchid lecture proved extremely popular.   (_____)

/ 5

Remove one letter from the first word and add it to the second word to make two new words. Do not rearrange the other letters. **Either** mark the letter that moves on the answer sheet, **or** write the two new words on the lines.

Example: coast   try   (<u>cost</u>)   (<u>tray</u>)

62. botch   pat   (_____)   (_____)

63. plain   host   (_____)   (_____)

64. board   boy   (_____)   (_____)

65. solid   wry   (_____)   (_____)

66. defer   let   (_____)   (_____)

/ 5

Find the pair of letters that continues each sequence in the best way. Use the alphabet to help you.

A B C D E F G H I J K L M N O P Q R S T U V W X Y Z

Example: GB   FD   EF   DH   (<u>CJ</u>)

67. FC   BH   EM   AR   DW   (_____)

68. OC   MF   LI   LL   MO   (_____)

69. VP   TS   PX   JE   BN   (_____)

70. YK   SN   VR   PW   SC   (_____)

71. HP   JO   KO   KP   JR   (_____)

/ 5

> Read the information carefully, then use it to answer the question that follows.

72. Chris, Adnan, Rory, Courtney and Suki competed in a go-kart race. Rory reached the end of the course before Chris, and there were 1.5 seconds between them. Chris finished in half the time Adnan did. Suki wasn't last. The fastest time was 1 minute 12 seconds. Adnan's time was 2 minutes 28 seconds.

If these statements are true, only one of the sentences below **cannot** be true. Which one?

A Suki and Courtney came joint first.
B Adnan was slower than Courtney.
C Adnan and Suki finished in the same time.
D Courtney beat Rory.
E Chris had the second slowest time.

73. Willow, Brayden, Joey, Amara and Uriah are making pancakes. They have four toppings to choose from: sugar, bananas, strawberries and maple syrup. Joey and Amara put strawberries on their pancakes. Brayden avoids the maple syrup, but he adds more toppings than Uriah. Willow doesn't eat fruit. Amara ends up with sugar, strawberries and bananas. Joey sees Willow put maple syrup on her pancake and decides to do the same. Uriah has the same as Amara, minus the strawberries.

If these statements are true, only one of the sentences below **must** be true. Which one?

A Amara has fewer toppings than Joey.
B Everyone puts sugar on their pancakes.
C Willow and Joey have the same amount of toppings.
D Willow has fewer toppings than anyone else.
E Maple syrup was the least popular topping.

/ 2

> Find the number that continues each sequence in the best way.
>
> **Example: 11, 22, 33, 44, (55)**

74. **32, 30, 26, 18, (_____)**

75. **48, 2, 24, 8, 12, 32, (_____)**

76. **3, 15, 60, 180, 360, (_____)**

77. **8, 40, 56, 64, 68, 70, (_____)**

78. **32, 4, 26, 12, 20, 36, (_____)**

79. **95, 91, 82, 66, 41, (_____)**

80. **12, 31, 48, 61, 72, (_____)**

/ 7

Total   / 80

End of Test

Assessment Test 1

Assessment Test 2

Answer Sheets

Allow 60 minutes to do this test and work as quickly and as carefully as you can.

You can print **multiple-choice answer sheets** for these questions from our website — go to cgpbooks.co.uk/11plus/answer-sheets or scan the QR code on the right. If you'd prefer to answer the questions on the page, just follow the instructions in the question.

Mark a word from the first set, followed by a word from the second set, that go together to form a new word.

Example: (<u>sun</u> shine hot)   (tree <u>flower</u> grass)   (the new word is 'sunflower')

---

1. (stub air fan)   (attic born fair)

2. (stare bore rear)   (range dome ring)

3. (bur are inter)   (fear sting rest)

4. (dial reel asp)   (act halt ate)

5. (bare since line)   (ear rely rage)

/ 5

The number codes for three of these four words are listed in a random order. Work out the code to answer the questions.

FRET   SORT   ORES   ROTS

1362   4156   2316

6. Find the code for the word **ORES**.   (_____)

7. Find the code for the word **SOFT**.   (_____)

8. Find the word that has the number code **6352**.   (_____)

/ 3

The number codes for three of these four words are listed in a random order. Work out the code to answer the questions.

INTO   NODE   DIRT   REND

2367   3471   6542

9. Find the code for the word **REND**.   (_____)

10. Find the code for the word **TONE**.   (_____)

11. Find the word that has the number code **3614**.   (_____)

/ 3

Mark the word outside the brackets that has a similar meaning to the words in both sets of brackets.

Example: (pledge promise) (execute enact) contract inflict <u>commit</u> affirm do

12. (stratagem intrigue) (patch area) realm scheme plot artifice tract

13. (conclusion finding) (subtraction removal) demise detraction deduction discount diagnosis

14. (countless abundant) (host crowd) company horde manifold legion squadron

15. (peninsula headland) (shawl cloak) cape bill neck mantle wrap

16. (restraint manacle) (impede inhibit) bar fetter cuff hold curb

/ 5

Each question uses a different code. Use the alphabet to help you work out the answer to each question.

A B C D E F G H I J K L M N O P Q R S T U V W X Y Z

Example: If the code for **LINE** is **NKPG**, what is the code for **FOUR**? (<u>HQWT</u>)

17. If the code for **PLACE** is **KOZXV**, what is the code for **TOUTS**? (_____)

18. If the code for **ROUND** is **SMXJI**, what is **QPLOR** the code for? (_____)

19. If the code for **HUNCH** is **GVQHO**, what is **QPDXA** the code for? (_____)

20. If the code for **FLAIR** is **IJDGU**, what is the code for **COMET**? (_____)

21. If the code for **PLINTH** is **LJIPXN**, what is the code for **SPRINT**? (_____)

22. If the code for **WAGER** is **ZXICS**, what is **BBCPT** the code for? (_____)

23. If the code for **TIMING** is **RJMGOG**, what is **ZSIEIT** the code for? (_____)

/ 7

Find the word that completes the third pair of words so that it follows the same pattern as the first two pairs.

Example: agility tag unleash sun operate (<u>top</u>)

24. swing twine frown growl aloof (_____)

25. pepperoni pen lollipops lop bimonthly (_____)

26. unwitting nit oftenness fen epidurals (_____)

27. snootiness son transcript tar inexplicit (_____)

28. didgeridoo ode breathless set palindrome (_____)

/ 5

Carry on to the next question → →

Assessment Test 2

In each sentence below a four-letter word is hidden at the end of one word and the start of the next. **Either** mark the part of the sentence that contains the hidden word on the answer sheet, **or** write the hidden word on the line.

Example: I get a headac<u>he at</u> night. (<u>heat</u>)

29. My brother Tony requested extra cheese during dinner. (_____)

30. New homes occasionally have surprisingly large building defects. (_____)

31. Ravenous eagles flew down and inspected the provisions. (_____)

32. You must discover some reason behind the incident. (_____)

33. Somehow the hapless librarian keeps losing library books. (_____)

/ 5

Remove one letter from the first word and add it to the second word to make two new words. Do not rearrange the other letters. **Either** mark the letter that moves on the answer sheet, **or** write the two new words on the lines.

Example: coast   try   (<u>cost</u>) (<u>tray</u>)

34. forty   fling   (_____) (_____)

35. gland   ban   (_____) (_____)

36. spoilt   rate   (_____) (_____)

37. corpse   pity   (_____) (_____)

38. resign   dire   (_____) (_____)

/ 5

Find the number that completes the final set of numbers in the same way as the first two sets.

Example: 10 (50) 5   3 (18) 6   12 (<u>48</u>) 4

39. 17 (7) 25   14 (6) 22   5 (_____) 7

40. 12 (35) 5   16 (64) 8   13 (_____) 4

41. 42 (10) 7   63 (12) 9   80 (_____) 8

42. 7 (4) 9   5 (2) 3   6 (_____) 18

43. 7 (25) 12   2 (16) 6   19 (_____) 22

44. 4 (25) 3   9 (19) 1   4 (_____) 2

/ 6

> Read the information carefully, then use it to answer the question that follows.

45. Christian, Marcel, Hasim, Eve and Rana were practising taking penalties against a goalkeeper. They each took twelve penalties. Eve scored twice as many penalties as Marcel. Hasim and Christian scored seven penalties between them. The goalkeeper saved four of Rana's shots, and she missed the goal five times. Marcel scored two more penalties than Hasim. Eve was the only person who scored more than half her penalties.

    If these statements are true, only one of the sentences below **cannot** be true. Which one?

    A Hasim scored the fewest penalties.
    B Christian scored more penalties than Hasim.
    C Rana scored more penalties than Christian.
    D Eve scored more penalties than Marcel and Hasim combined.
    E Marcel scored six penalties.

46. Sujatha, Mei, Darren, Abigail and Landon agreed to meet in the park at 2 pm, but they all arrived at different times. Sujatha was the only person who arrived early. Landon arrived at 2.25 pm. Darren arrived 20 minutes after Sujatha. The last person arrived 35 minutes after the first person. Abigail was twice as late as Darren. Mei arrived after Landon.

    If these statements are true, only one of the sentences below **must** be true. Which one?

    A Mei arrived after Abigail.
    B Darren arrived before Mei.
    C Landon was the third person to arrive.
    D Abigail was the last person to arrive.
    E Sujatha arrived at 1.55 pm.

/ 2

> Find the missing number to complete each sum.
>
> **Example:** $20 + 7 = 9 \times (\underline{\;3\;})$

47. $6 \times 11 \div 3 - 14 = 48 \div 8 + (\underline{\qquad})$

48. $72 \div 8 + 23 - 17 = 72 \div 6 + (\underline{\qquad})$

49. $63 \div 9 \times 4 - 19 = (\underline{\qquad}) \times 3 - 21$

50. $5 \times 12 \div 4 + 34 = 11 \times (\underline{\qquad}) - 6$

51. $11 \times 9 \div 3 - 15 + 43 = (\underline{\qquad}) \times 5 + 16$

52. $132 \div 11 \times 7 - 18 + 55 = 99 \div 9 \times (\underline{\qquad})$

53. $54 \div 6 \times 9 - 17 + 8 = 42 \div (\underline{\qquad}) \times 12$

/ 7

Carry on to the next question → →

Assessment Test 2

Find the number that continues each sequence in the best way.

Example: 11, 22, 33, 44, (_55_)

54. **23, 41, 53, 59, 59, (_____)**

55. **1, 1, 3, 12, 9, 144, (_____)**

56. **1, 7, 35, 105, (_____)**

57. **37, 45, 82, 127, (_____)**

58. **2, 48, 2, 12, 6, 6, (_____)**

/ 5

Mark two words, one from each set of brackets, that have the most opposite meaning.

Example: (<u>wide</u> large high)   (long <u>narrow</u> short)

59. (faltering unreliable tentative)   (categorical honourable resistant)

60. (imperceptible unassuming indistinct)   (plausible palpable characteristic)

61. (skewed widespread anomalous)   (typical rigid expected)

62. (lie contention conjecture)   (composure foundation certitude)

63. (despondency calamity aggravation)   (mindfulness disposition euphoria)

/ 5

Read the information carefully, then use it to answer the question that follows.

64. Gav, Nari, Joe, Isla and Yasmin are at a music festival with five stages, each hosting a different act.

   Nari and Yasmin are the only people who don't watch 'Soundburst' on Stage 2. Everyone except Joe watches the act on Stage 1. The timings of the acts on stages 3 and 5 clash, so Isla and Yasmin watch 'Power Pair' on Stage 3. After watching 'Bandit Boys' on Stage 5, Gav, Nari and Joe watch the act on Stage 4. Everyone except Isla watches 'Blue Tigers'. 'Land of Noise' are playing on Stage 1.

   Who watches the **most** acts?   (_____)

65. Sarai, Tara, Amos, Viv and Will are spending the weekend at an outdoor activity centre.

   There are six activities on offer at the centre: three of them take place in the centre (on-site), and three take place in a nearby location (off-site). Tara does all the off-site activities. Everyone goes kayaking. Will and Tara go mountain biking while everyone else does quad biking. Sarai and Viv do all the on-site activities. Amos and Tara go canyoning while the others do archery. Everyone except Tara goes rock climbing. The off-site activities are mountain biking, kayaking and canyoning.

   Who does the **fewest** activities?   (_____)

/ 2

Assessment Test 2

Find the three-letter word that completes the word in capital letters, and finishes the sentence in a sensible way.

Example: They waited on the **PLATM** for their train. (___FOR___)

66. On safari, we saw lions in their natural **HAAT**. (_____)

67. Millie was **INNANT** at being blamed for the mess. (_____)

68. The hastily scrawled note was totally **ILIBLE**. (_____)

69. The motorway runs **ADJNT** to the train tracks. (_____)

70. "Do not harm us, I **BECH** you!" the king pleaded. (_____)

/ 5

Mark two words, one from each set of brackets, that complete the sentence in the most sensible way.

Example: **Bird** is to (wood   twig   <u>nest</u>) as **bee** is to (buzz   flower   <u>hive</u>).

71. **Pail** is to (bucket   contain   fill) as **tongs** is to (spatula   grip   reach).

72. **Delectable** is to (delightful   unsavoury   irate) as **ardent** is to (vapid   poignant   lukewarm).

73. **Emaciated** is to (health   nourished   food) as **pasty** is to (sunlight   skin   ashen).

74. **Tanner** is to (leather   skin   fur) as **tailor** is to (dress   material   clothes).

75. **Ravine** is to (crater   ditch   canyon) as **stream** is to (current   estuary   river).

/ 5

Find the pair of letters that continues each sequence in the best way.
Use the alphabet to help you.

A B C D E F G H I J K L M N O P Q R S T U V W X Y Z

Example: GB   FD   EF   DH   (___CJ___)

76. TG   SF   SI   TH   VK   (_____)

77. EO   WU   QX   MD   KG   (_____)

78. JX   MZ   QF   TP   XD   (_____)

79. ED   MY   PE   NZ   GF   (_____)

80. PX   UI   LP   QS   HR   (_____)

/ 5

Total   / 80

End of Test

Assessment Test 2

Assessment Test 3

Answer Sheets

Allow 60 minutes to do this test and work as quickly and as carefully as you can.

You can print **multiple-choice answer sheets** for these questions from our website — go to cgpbooks.co.uk/11plus/answer-sheets or scan the QR code on the right. If you'd prefer to answer the questions on the page, just follow the instructions in the question.

Find the missing number to complete each sum.

Example: $20 + 7 = 9 \times ($ _3_ $)$

1. $96 \div 8 + 73 - 27 + 16 = 9 \times 9 - ($ _____ $)$

2. $8 \times 9 \div 6 + 47 - 21 = 132 \div ($ _____ $) + 27$

3. $108 \div 9 \times 3 + 18 + 57 = ($ _____ $) \times 9 + 21$

4. $56 \div 7 \times 11 + 97 - 72 = 24 \times ($ _____ $) + 17$

5. $12 \times 12 \div 8 + 77 - 38 = ($ _____ $) \times 4 - 19$

/ 5

Find the letter that will finish the first word and start the second word of each pair. The same letter must be used for both pairs. **Either** mark the letter on the answer sheet, **or** write it on the line.

Example: cam (?) alm   bli (?) ole   (__p__)

6. cla (?) arn   slo (?) ear   (_____)

7. flo (?) ar   sho (?) ach   (_____)

8. hel (?) alt   sea (?) ark   (_____)

9. glu (?) out   pin (?) ist   (_____)

10. to (?) ust   her (?) il   (_____)

/ 5

Each letter stands for a number. Work out the answer to each sum as a letter.

Example: $A = 3 \quad B = 6 \quad C = 7 \quad D = 10 \quad E = 12$ $A + D - C = ($ __B__ $)$

11. $A = 3 \quad B = 8 \quad C = 20 \quad D = 23 \quad E = 69$ $E \div D \times A \times B - E + C = ($ _____ $)$

12. $A = 2 \quad B = 5 \quad C = 12 \quad D = 22 \quad E = 30$ $B \times C \div E \times D - A - C = ($ _____ $)$

13. $A = 3 \quad B = 6 \quad C = 8 \quad D = 9 \quad E = 22$ $C \times D \div B \times A - E - B = ($ _____ $)$

14. $A = 4 \quad B = 5 \quad C = 6 \quad D = 12 \quad E = 18$ $C \times A \times B \div D + D - E = ($ _____ $)$

15. $A = 6 \quad B = 8 \quad C = 9 \quad D = 12 \quad E = 25$ $B \times A \div D \times C - E + A - C = ($ _____ $)$

/ 5

In each sentence below a four-letter word is hidden at the end of one word and the start of the next. **Either** mark the part of the sentence that contains the hidden word on the answer sheet, **or** write the hidden word on the line.

Example: I get a heada<u>che at</u> night.   (___heat___)

16. The unwelcome guest is leaving immediately after dinner.   (_____)

17. Global meat production is predicted to decline gradually.   (_____)

18. Surely celebrities have occasional flaws like everyone else?   (_____)

19. The fiendishly hard maze always confuses the competitors.   (_____)

20. Hattie wishes you would stop using her conditioner.   (_____)

/ 5

The words in the second set follow the same pattern as the words in the first set. Find the missing word to complete the second set.

Example: blow (own) nap   clan (___and___) dust

21. cheer (hire) third   gates (_____) smoke

22. louse (soul) slows   pylon (_____) slant

23. spare (seat) taste   odour (_____) waged

24. lapse (pale) apple   untie (_____) foils

25. losses (sole) pollen   bistro (_____) outlaw

/ 5

Find the three-letter word that completes the word in capital letters, and finishes the sentence in a sensible way.

Example: They waited on the **PLATM** for their train. (___FOR___)

26. He plodded through his forgotten town, dreaming of **FAAY** places.   (_____)

27. After Mr Gupta retired, Mrs Rice took up the **MLE** of headteacher.   (_____)

28. The marauding warriors **PILED** the town, damaging many buildings.   (_____)

29. The leisure complex is equipped with every **AITY** you could think of.   (_____)

30. He boasts of his **PESS** on the rugby pitch, but I haven't seen him play.   (_____)

/ 5

Carry on to the next question → →

Assessment Test 3

The number codes for three of these four words are listed in a random order. Work out the code to answer the questions.

VEST   EVIL   LINT   TINS

4372   5634   2371

31. Find the code for the word **VEST**.   (_____)

32. Find the code for the word **ISLE**.   (_____)

33. Find the word that has the number code **1342**.   (_____)

/ 3

The number codes for three of these four words are listed in a random order. Work out the code to answer the questions.

OMIT   INTO   NOSE   STEM

5713   2451   6274

34. Find the code for the word **OMIT**.   (_____)

35. Find the code for the word **SITE**.   (_____)

36. Find the word that has the number code **7425**.   (_____)

/ 3

Mark two words, one from each set of brackets, that have the most similar meaning.

Example: (excited hopeful <u>sad</u>)   (angry <u>unhappy</u> lucky)

37. (maim sully vilify)   (soil obliterate corrode)

38. (defeatist detached funereal)   (inadequate inconsolable pessimistic)

39. (fabricate venerate bestow)   (elaborate confer adorn)

40. (fidelity vitality shrewdness)   (sleight finesse acumen)

41. (unprecedented fateful seminal)   (preliminary influential pernicious)

/ 5

Find the number that continues each sequence in the best way.

Example: 11, 22, 33, 44, (_55_)

42. **1890, 210, 30, 6, (_____)**

43. **154, 105, 69, 44, 28, (_____)**

44. **33, 42, 38, 39, 45, 36, (_____)**

45. **6, 25, 48, 77, 108, (_____)**

46. **3, 128, 192, 219, 227, (_____)**

/ 5

Mark the pair of letters that completes each sentence in the most sensible way. Use the alphabet to help you.

A B C D E F G H I J K L M N O P Q R S T U V W X Y Z

Example: DK is to **FM** as **PT** is to   (RS   <u>RV</u>   QV   QW   RU).

47. **NC** is to **YY** as **DT** is to   (NQ   OO   PQ   PP   OP).

48. **FI** is to **RU** as **DY** is to   (CV   BW   BX   AV   WB).

49. **ET** is to **UL** as **KB** is to   (AT   AU   XS   ZS   ZT).

50. **TW** is to **FL** as **BH** is to   (OW   MX   OX   NW   NX).

51. **QJ** is to **HS** as **CX** is to   (GT   UF   TG   FU   VE).

/ 5

Three of the words in each list are linked. Mark the two words that are not related to these three.

Example: jump   hop   <u>stroll</u>   leap   <u>hike</u>

52. psychiatrist   impressionist   receptionist   protagonist   journalist

53. encumber   saddle   thwart   burden   furnish

54. surgery   refuge   sanctuary   asylum   infirmary

55. susceptible   pliable   tractable   flexible   dispensable

56. octopus   whale   earthworm   jellyfish   shark

/ 5

Each question uses a different code. Use the alphabet to help you work out the answer to each question.

A B C D E F G H I J K L M N O P Q R S T U V W X Y Z

Example: If the code for **LINE** is **NKPG**, what is the code for **FOUR**? (<u>HQWT</u>)

57. If the code for **CAMEL** is **XZNVO**, what is **UORMG** the code for?   (_____)

58. If the code for **WATCH** is **RXSDK**, what is the code for **BUSHY**?   (_____)

59. If the code for **GRAZE** is **IPDWI**, what is **DMRPX** the code for?   (_____)

60. If the code for **PROFIT** is **JNMFKX**, what is **YZGBNI** the code for? (_____)

61. If the code for **AGENCY** is **YKBQYA**, what is the code for **SPIRIT**? (_____)

/ 5

Carry on to the next question → →

Assessment Test 3

> Read the information carefully, then use it to answer the question that follows.

62. Oscar, Fiona, Mia, Poppy and Amad have all been watching Shakespeare plays at their local theatre.

The theatre staged a different play every month, from January to May. Mia, Poppy and Oscar were the only ones who watched 'The Tempest' in February, but everyone watched 'Othello' in March. Four of the children watched the play in May. The first play to be performed was 'Hamlet', but only Amad saw it. Fiona watched 'Twelfth Night' and 'Othello' in consecutive months. Poppy missed 'Macbeth', but she did watch 'Twelfth Night' with Amad. Oscar and Mia missed the play in April.

Who watched the **most** plays?   (_____)

63. Simran, Dafydd, Millie, Jacob and Levi recently visited the Ancient History Museum.

The museum had five floors, and there was a different exhibit on each floor. Everyone except Levi and Millie visited the Americas exhibit on the third floor. Dafydd was the only child not to visit the Romans exhibit on the ground floor. Three of the children visited the exhibit on the first floor. Levi and Simran were the only children who visited the Ancient Greece exhibit, which was located on the floor directly above the Ancient Egypt exhibit. Only Jacob and Dafydd went to the Middle East exhibit, which was on the top floor. Jacob and Simran did not visit the Ancient Egypt exhibit.

Who visited the **fewest** exhibits?   (_____)

/ 2

> Mark the word outside the brackets that has a similar meaning to the words in both sets of brackets.
>
> **Example:** (pledge promise) (execute enact) contract inflict <u>commit</u> affirm do

64. (guide steer)   (experimental trial)   control pilot conduct test lead

65. (venture gamble) (conjecture theorise)   postulate wager surmise speculate bid

66. (pertinent apt)   (seize commandeer)   usurp opportune appropriate apposite exact

67. (intonation diction) (emphasis stress)   tone timbre delivery accent prominence

68. (bargain haggle)   (traverse clear)   barter cross hurdle settle negotiate

/ 5

> Find the number that completes the final set of numbers in the same way as the first two sets.
>
> **Example:** 10 (50) 5   3 (18) 6   12 (**48**) 4

69. 11 (2) 17   12 (3) 30   26 (_____) 30

70. 36 (12) 9   42 (18) 7   25 (_____) 5

71. 4 (7) 11   4 (6) 8   11 (_____) 13

72. 7 (9) 3   12 (22) 4   9 (_____) 8

73. 11 (72) 18   3 (25) 13   6 (_____) 8

/ 5

Find the word that completes the third pair of words so that it follows the same pattern as the first two pairs.

    Example: agility tag   unleash sun   operate (_____top_____)

74. accolades ace   aggrieved age   community (_____)

75. addiction din   efficient fit   breakaway (_____)

76. attestant tan   associate sat   musketeer (_____)

77. cameraman arm   retracted eat   authoring (_____)

78. tessellate set   stigmatist its   nominative (_____)

/ 5

Read the information carefully, then use it to answer the question that follows.

79. Eniola, Cass, Patrick, Keith and Sasha all recorded the amount of sleep they got over five nights, from Monday to Friday. Patrick slept for 38 hours in total. No one slept for more than 10 hours or fewer than 7 hours on any single night. Sasha slept for 9 hours on Monday, Tuesday and Wednesday. By the weekend, Keith had slept for 3 hours more than Eniola. Cass slept for at least 8 hours every night. Eniola got the fewest hours of sleep over the five nights.

If these statements are true, only one of the sentences below **must** be true. Which one?

A Over the five nights, Sasha got more sleep than Cass.
B Over the five nights, Patrick got more sleep than Sasha.
C Over the five nights, Cass got more sleep than Keith.
D Over the five nights, Sasha got more sleep than Keith.
E Over the five nights, Keith got more sleep than Cass.

80. Ruby, Alex, Gwen, Omar and Leo took part in an archery competition. They each had six shots. For each shot, they got fifty points if they hit the bullseye, twenty points if they hit anywhere else on the target, and zero points if they missed the target. Everyone hit the bullseye at least once. The winner scored 190 points. None of Omar's arrows missed the target, but he wasn't the winner. Alex scored twice as many points as Gwen. Leo hit the bullseye three times, and Alex hit it twice.

If these statements are true, only one of the sentences below **cannot** be true. Which one?

A Leo was the winner.
B Alex scored 160 points.
C Omar scored 180 points.
D Ruby finished second.
E Half of Gwen's arrows hit the target.

/ 2

Total   / 80

End of Test

Assessment Test 3

Answers

Section One — Making Words

Page 2 — Missing Letters

1) **o** — The new words are 'too', 'owe', 'ago' and 'odd'.
2) **h** — The new words are 'mash', 'hiss', 'cash' and 'hose'.
3) **r** — The new words are 'our', 'road', 'deer' and 'rank'.
4) **b** — The new words are 'swab', 'bold', 'comb' and 'boss'.
5) **e** — The new words are 'here', 'eats', 'die' and 'even'.
6) **d** — The new words are 'hood', 'dust', 'gold' and 'does'.
7) **e** — The new words are 'tee', 'end', 'gale' and 'eel'.
8) **g** — The new words are 'wig', 'got', 'rag' and 'guy'.
9) **l** — The new words are 'rail', 'lawn', 'real' and 'loot'.
10) **b** — The new words are 'hub', 'brow', 'job' and 'bulk'.
11) **s** — The new words are 'pass', 'sue', 'plus', and 'sigh'.
12) **k** — The new words are 'silk', 'kilt', 'ask' and 'kind'.
13) **s** — The new words are 'his', 'set', 'was' and 'such'.
14) **g** — The new words are 'rung', 'gown', 'wing' and 'grip'.
15) **d** — The new words are 'sand', 'did', 'cord' and 'done'.
16) **h** — The new words are 'path', 'hire', 'wish' and 'hail'.
17) **p** — The new words are 'weep', 'pill', 'step' and 'peep'.
18) **o** — The new words are 'trio', 'oath', 'polo' and 'oat'.
19) **y** — The new words are 'any', 'your', 'bay' and 'yelp'.
20) **n** — The new words are 'bean', 'nook', 'pain' and 'news'.

Page 3 — Missing Letters

1) **f** — The new words are 'half', 'fend', 'deaf' and 'fry'.
2) **r** — The new words are 'tier', 'rat', 'air' and 'rice'.
3) **l** — The new words are 'fail', 'lose', 'wool' and 'lift'.
4) **y** — The new words are 'deny', 'yell', 'tiny' and 'yowl'.
5) **w** — The new words are 'blew', 'wove', 'jaw' and 'waft'.
6) **n** — The new words are 'swan', 'nap', 'rain' and 'nigh'.
7) **r** — The new words are 'soar', 'rosy', 'seer' and 'rind'.
8) **f** — The new words are 'beef', 'fit', 'calf' and 'fix'.
9) **s** — The new words are 'has', 'seal', 'moss' and 'said'.
10) **c** — The new words are 'arc', 'car', 'disc' and 'cow'.
11) **d** — The new words are 'goad', 'dish', 'wild' and 'din'.
12) **e** — The new words are 'wane', 'eye', 'lame' and 'earn'.
13) **t** — The new words are 'whet', 'tour', 'foot' and 'tank'.
14) **w** — The new words are 'paw', 'wry', 'show' and 'word'.
15) **t** — The new words are 'heat', 'tap', 'must' and 'tub'.
16) **p** — The new words are 'warp', 'pour', 'swap' and 'pave'.
17) **l** — The new words are 'soul', 'lest', 'earl' and 'lain'.
18) **c** — The new words are 'chic', 'cape', 'zinc' and 'cook'.
19) **d** — The new words are 'clad', 'doe', 'wad' and 'dire'.
20) **m** — The new words are 'skim', 'mull', 'loom' and 'muse'.
21) **f** — The new words are 'waif', 'fawn', 'reef' and 'feel'.
22) **t** — The new words are 'spat', 'tag', 'moot' and 'taut'.

Page 4 — Move a Letter

1) **g** — The new words are 'sure' and 'frog'.
2) **a** — The new words are 'chin' and 'wait'.
3) **o** — The new words are 'pint' and 'soon'.
4) **w** — The new words are 'sing' and 'wall'.
5) **m** — The new words are 'char' and 'whom'.
6) **e** — The new words are 'suit' and 'least'.
7) **p** — The new words are 'seed' and 'reply'.
8) **l** — The new words are 'word' and 'plain'.
9) **w** — The new words are 'sift' and 'sewer'.
10) **i** — The new words are 'chef' and 'pilot'.
11) **l** — The new words are 'spit' and 'flour'.
12) **g** — The new words are 'rein' and 'tiger'.
13) **b** — The new words are 'road' and 'rebel'.
14) **r** — The new words are 'font' and 'rapt'.
15) **c** — The new words are 'fore' and 'acid'.
16) **t** — The new words are 'sand' and 'vital'.
17) **v** — The new words are 'care' and 'gravy'.
18) **p** — The new words are 'lease' and 'spend'.
19) **c** — The new words are 'ream' and 'score'.
20) **m** — The new words are 'thee' and 'times'.

Page 5 — Move a Letter

1) **p** — The new words are 'relay' and 'rapid'.
2) **n** — The new words are 'rage' and 'spring'.
3) **h** — The new words are 'trust' and 'though'.
4) **l** — The new words are 'fairy' and 'flight'.
5) **f** — The new words are 'reuse' and 'flair'.
6) **e** — The new words are 'crate' and 'career'.
7) **c** — The new words are 'pith' and 'backed'.
8) **e** — The new words are 'writ' and 'below'.
9) **a** — The new words are 'bout' and 'launch'.
10) **j** — The new words are 'aunt' and 'fjord'.
11) **r** — The new words are 'fiend' and 'pretty'.
12) **y** — The new words are 'canon' and 'honey'.
13) **s** — The new words are 'deign' and 'spent'.
14) **u** — The new words are 'gild' and 'debut'.
15) **t** — The new words are 'sage' and 'facet'.
16) **v** — The new words are 'drier' and 'seven'.
17) **f** — The new words are 'rile' and 'defer'.
18) **o** — The new words are 'avid' and 'court'.
19) **k** — The new words are 'spar' and 'linked'.
20) **w** — The new words are 'oven' and 'gawp'.
21) **n** — The new words are 'bled' and 'corner'.
22) **i** — The new words are 'bran' and 'poise'.

Page 6 — Hidden Word

1) **spat her** — The hidden word is 'path'.
2) **attract some** — The hidden word is 'acts'.
3) **felt ripples** — The hidden word is 'trip'.
4) **follow orders** — The hidden word is 'word'.
5) **entire armies** — The hidden word is 'rear'.
6) **ribbon edge** — The hidden word is 'bone'.
7) **My third** — The hidden word is 'myth'.
8) **ski with** — The hidden word is 'kiwi'.
9) **due to** — The hidden word is 'duet'.
10) **bronze statue** — The hidden word is 'zest'.
11) **black ink** — The hidden word is 'kink'.
12) **I dolloped** — The hidden word is 'idol'.
13) **video mentioned** — The hidden word is 'omen'.
14) **fixes watches** — The hidden word is 'swat'.
15) **Your gecko** — The hidden word is 'urge'.
16) **snowy owl** — The hidden word is 'yowl'.
17) **hyper kangaroos** — The hidden word is 'perk'.

18) **system it** — The hidden word is 'emit'.

19) **with elm** — The hidden word is 'helm'.

20) **lava leaked** — The hidden word is 'vale'.

Page 7 — Hidden Word

1) **cinema ultimately** — The hidden word is 'maul'.

2) **yourself little** — The hidden word is 'flit'.

3) **who axed** — The hidden word is 'hoax'.

4) **gourmet cheese** — The hidden word is 'etch'.

5) **visit actual** — The hidden word is 'tact'.

6) **A midge** — The hidden word is 'amid'.

7) **before applying** — The hidden word is 'reap'.

8) **gap either** — The hidden word is 'gape'.

9) **saw rye** — The hidden word is 'awry'.

10) **saw him** — The hidden word is 'whim'.

11) **have to** — The hidden word is 'veto'.

12) **circus performers** — The hidden word is 'cusp'.

13) **Milo uttered** — The hidden word is 'lout'.

14) **a crevice** — The hidden word is 'acre'.

15) **vigil tomorrow** — The hidden word is 'gilt'.

16) **bid everyone** — The hidden word is 'bide'.

17) **occur twice** — The hidden word is 'curt'.

18) **forum aims** — The hidden word is 'maim'.

19) **You stand** — The hidden word is 'oust'.

20) **happy reaction** — The hidden word is 'pyre'.

21) **playing lutes** — The hidden word is 'glut'.

22) **All audience** — The hidden word is 'laud'.

Page 8 — Find the Missing Word

1) **BIN** — The complete word is CABINET.

2) **EBB** — The complete word is PEBBLE.

3) **ODE** — The complete word is MODERN.

4) **OPT** — The complete word is ADOPTED.

5) **NIB** — The complete word is MINIBUS.

6) **CRY** — The complete word is CRYSTAL.

7) **DEW** — The complete word is SIDEWAYS.

8) **GET** — The complete word is FIDGETY.

9) **YOU** — The complete word is LAYOUT.

10) **USE** — The complete word is MUSEUM.

11) **VAT** — The complete word is EXCAVATED.

12) **NOT** — The complete word is ANOTHER.

13) **AWE** — The complete word is SEAWEED.

14) **MAR** — The complete word is ROSEMARY.

15) **VET** — The complete word is VELVETY.

16) **LET** — The complete word is PALETTE.

17) **HIM** — The complete word is SHIMMER.

18) **ICE** — The complete word is LATTICE.

19) **LIE** — The complete word is DISBELIEF.

20) **SIR** — The complete word is DESIRABLE.

Page 9 — Find the Missing Word

1) **FUN** — The complete word is MALFUNCTION.

2) **KIT** — The complete word is SKITTISH.

3) **SUM** — The complete word is ASSUMED.

4) **KIN** — The complete word is UNKINDLY.

5) **DUE** — The complete word is SUBDUED.

6) **YES** — The complete word is EYESIGHT.

7) **SUE** — The complete word is ENSUE.

8) **RUT** — The complete word is RUTHLESS.

9) **WAD** — The complete word is NOWADAYS.

10) **THY** — The complete word is AMETHYST.

11) **ERR** — The complete word is OVERREACT.

12) **ZIP** — The complete word is MARZIPAN.

13) **GEM** — The complete word is JUDGEMENT.

14) **ROD** — The complete word is PRODUCE.

15) **BAD** — The complete word is FORBADE.

16) **PLY** — The complete word is IMPLYING.

17) **AIL** — The complete word is PREVAILING.

18) **VIE** — The complete word is SERVIETTE.

19) **WIN** — The complete word is HARROWING.

20) **FIN** — The complete word is AFFINITY.

21) **IRK** — The complete word is QUIRKY.

22) **DUO** — The complete word is ARDUOUS.

Page 10 — Use a Rule to Make a Word

1) **duel** — Take letter 4 from the first word, followed by letter 1 from the second word, then letters 2 and 3 from the first word.

2) **ease** — Take letter 1 from the second word, followed by letters 2 and 3 from the first word, then letter 4 from the second word.

3) **pelt** — Take letters 2, 5 and 4 from the second word, followed by letter 2 from the first word.

4) **hoot** — Take letter 2 from the first word, followed by letters 4 and 2 from the second word, then letter 4 from the first word.

5) **coil** — Take letters 3 and 2 from the first word, followed by letters 2 and 3 from the second word.

6) **swan** — Take letter 5 from the second word, followed by letter 5 from the first word, then letter 3 from the second word, then letter 3 from the first word.

7) **rife** — Take letter 4 from the first word, followed by letters 4 and 1 from the second word, then letter 3 from the first word.

8) **tilt** — Take letter 1 from the second word, followed by letters 4 and 5 from the first word, then letter 5 from the second word.

9) **bawl** — Take letters 2 and 1 from the second word, followed by letter 4 from the first word, then letter 3 from the second word.

10) **pink** — Take letter 3 from the second word, followed by letter 2 from the first word, then letter 1 from the second word, then letter 3 from the first word.

11) **unit** — Take letters 2 and 1 from the second word, followed by letters 2 and 3 from the first word.

12) **what** — Take letter 4 from the second word, followed by letter 2 from the first word, then letter 3 from the second word, then letter 4 from the first word.

13) **exit** — Take letter 2 from the first word, followed by letters 3, 4 and 1 from the second word.

14) **faux** — Take letter 1 from the first word, followed by letter 2 from the second word, then letters 3 and 4 from the first word.

15) **lead** — Take letters 2 and 4 from the first word, followed by letter 3 from the second word, then letter 3 from the first word.

16) **wrap** — Take letter 3 from the second word, followed by letter 2 from the first word, then letter 2 from the second word, then letter 4 from the first word.

17) **twee** — Take letters 1, 3 and 4 from the first word, followed by letter 2 from the second word.

18) **snub** — Take letter 5 from the first word, followed by letters 3, 2 and 1 from the second word.

19) **cost** — Take letter 4 from the second word, followed by letters 2 and 4 from the first word, then letter 5 from the second word.

20) **tile** — Take letter 2 from the second word, followed by letters 2 and 5 from the first word, then letter 3 from the second word.

Page 11 — Use a Rule to Make a Word

1) **next** — Take letter 5 from the first word, followed by letters 5 and 3 from the second word, then letter 1 from the first word.

2) **drum** — Take letters 3 and 5 from the second word, followed by letters 3 and 2 from the first word.

3) **reek** — Take letters 2 and 4 from the second word, followed by letter 4 from the first word, then letter 3 from the second word.

4) **icon** — Take letter 4 from the second word, followed by letter 1 from the first word, then letter 3 from the second word, then letter 3 from the first word.

5) **kiln** — Take letter 4 from the second word, followed by letters 3 and 2 from the first word, then letter 3 from the second word.

6) **glee** — Take letter 2 from the second word, followed by letters 3 and 2 from the first word, then letter 5 from the second word.

7) **hewn** — Take letter 1 from the first word, followed by letters 2, 3 and 1 from the second word.

8) **slap** — Take letters 4, 3 and 2 from the second word, followed by letter 4 from the first word.

9) **zone** — Take letter 1 from the first word, followed by letters 2 and 5 from the second word, then letter 2 from the first word.

10) **glut** — Take letters 1 and 4 from the second word, followed by letters 2 and 5 from the first word.

11) **gait** — Take letter 3 from the second word, followed by letters 4 and 1 from the first word, then letter 1 from the second word.

12) **yolk** — Take letter 5 from the first word, followed by letters 3 and 2 from the second word, then letter 4 from the first word.

13) **calm** — Take letter 6 from the first word, followed by letter 6 from the second word, then letter 4 from the first word, then letter 3 from the second word.

14) **rune** — Take letters 3 and 4 from the first word, followed by letters 5 and 4 from the second word.

15) **toad** — Take letters 1 and 2 from the second word, followed by letters 1 and 4 from the first word.

16) **bald** — Take letter 3 from the second word, followed by letters 5 and 1 from the first word, then letter 1 from the second word.

17) **flog** — Take letter 1 from the second word, followed by letters 1 and 5 from the first word, then letter 5 from the second word.

18) **spar** — Take letter 4 from the first word, followed by letters 2 and 3 from the second word, then letter 1 from the first word.

19) **bray** — Take letters 1, 3 and 2 from the second word, followed by letter 6 from the first word.

20) **pact** — Take letters 3 and 4 from the first word, followed by letters 1 and 6 from the second word.

21) **mire** — Take letters 4 and 5 from the first word, followed by letters 4 and 5 from the second word.

22) **lapel** — Take letter 1 from the first word, followed by letter 2 from the second word, then letters 3 and 4 from the first word, then letter 1 from the second word.

Page 12 — Compound Words

1) **inhabitants** — 'inhabitants' is the only word that can be made.

2) **lovestruck** — 'lovestruck' is the only word that can be made.

3) **allowing** — 'allowing' is the only word that can be made.

4) **wavering** — 'wavering' is the only word that can be made.

5) **constables** — 'constables' is the only word that can be made.

6) **equalled** — 'equalled' is the only word that can be made.

7) **weightier** — 'weightier' is the only word that can be made.

8) **brandish** — 'brandish' is the only word that can be made.

9) **denounce** — 'denounce' is the only word that can be made.

10) **errant** — 'errant' is the only word that can be made.

11) **office** — 'office' is the only word that can be made.

12) **massaged** — 'massaged' is the only word that can be made.

13) **heartrending** — 'heartrending' is the only word that can be made.

14) **grimaced** — 'grimaced' is the only word that can be made.

15) **feathers** — 'feathers' is the only word that can be made.

16) **readjust** — 'readjust' is the only word that can be made.

17) **buttoning** — 'buttoning' is the only word that can be made.

18) **determine** — 'determine' is the only word that can be made.

19) **crumbled** — 'crumbled' is the only word that can be made.

20) **honesty** — 'honesty' is the only word that can be made.

Page 13 — Compound Words

1) **noticed** — 'noticed' is the only word that can be made.

2) **riddance** — 'riddance' is the only word that can be made.

3) **comedies** — 'comedies' is the only word that can be made.

4) **verbally** — 'verbally' is the only word that can be made.

5) **reinspire** — 'reinspire' is the only word that can be made.

6) **usability** — 'usability' is the only word that can be made.

7) **dabbled** — 'dabbled' is the only word that can be made.

8) **kindred** — 'kindred' is the only word that can be made.

9) **therein** — 'therein' is the only word that can be made.

10) **hasten** — 'hasten' is the only word that can be made.

11) **earthen** — 'earthen' is the only word that can be made.

12) **scarcity** — 'scarcity' is the only word that can be made.

13) **hallowed** — 'hallowed' is the only word that can be made.

14) **permeating** — 'permeating' is the only word that can be made.

15) **doused** — 'doused' is the only word that can be made.

16) **lacerate** — 'lacerate' is the only word that can be made.

17) **lithe** — 'lithe' is the only word that can be made.

18) **flagrant** — 'flagrant' is the only word that can be made.

19) **fathomed** — 'fathomed' is the only word that can be made.

20) **candour** — 'candour' is the only word that can be made.

21) **pallor** — 'pallor' is the only word that can be made.

22) **penchant** — 'penchant' is the only word that can be made.

Page 14 — Complete a Word Pair

1) **sheep** — The last letter of the word moves forward two places along the alphabet.

2) **fan** — Remove letters 1, 2, 5, 6, 7 and 8, leaving the remaining letters in the order 3, 4, 9.

3) **urn** — Remove letters 1, 3, 4, 6 and 7, leaving the remaining letters in the order 2, 5, 8.

4) **chap** — The second letter of the word moves backward four places along the alphabet.

5) **tar** — Rearrange letters 2, 3, 7 in the order 3, 2, 7.

6) **one** — Rearrange letters 2, 4, 6 in the order 6, 4, 2.

7) **sue** — Rearrange letters 1, 3, 5 in the order 5, 3, 1.

8) **dug** — Rearrange letters 3, 6 and 9 in the order 6, 3, 9.

9) **bit** — Remove letters 1, 4, 5 and 7, leaving the remaining letters in the order 2, 3, 6.

10) **sea** — Rearrange letters 3, 4, 6 in the order 4, 6, 3.

11) **ore** — Rearrange letters 2, 6, 7 in the order 2, 7, 6.

12) **aid** — Rearrange letters 4, 7 and 8 in the order 4, 8 7.

13) **eat** — Rearrange letters 1, 2, 4 in the order 4, 1 2.

14) **met** — Rearrange letters 3, 5, 8 in the order 5, 8, 3.

15) **vat** — Rearrange letters 1, 3, 7 in the order 3, 1, 7.

16) **foe** — Rearrange letters 2, 5, 7 in the order 5, 2, 7.

17) **lob** — Rearrange letters 1, 2, 8 in the order 2, 8, 1.

18) **him** — Rearrange letters 1, 5, 7 in the order 1, 7, 5.

19) **opt** — Rearrange letters 2, 4, 6 in the order 4, 2, 6.

20) **bud** — Rearrange letters 2, 4, 9 in the order 4, 2, 9.

Page 15 — Complete a Word Pair

1) **jar** — Rearrange letters 1, 4, 6 in the order 1, 6, 4.

2) **veil** — The first and third letters of the word move backward three places along the alphabet.

3) **kin** — Remove letters 3, 4, 5, 6, 7, 9 and 10, leaving the remaining letters in the order 1, 2, 8.

4) **tut** — Rearrange letters 4, 8, 9 in the order 9, 8, 4.

5) **wad** — Rearrange letters 1, 3, 6 in the order 3, 6, 1.

6) **hub** — Rearrange letters 1, 3, 6 in the order 1, 6, 3.

7) **vie** — Rearrange letters 2, 3, 5 in the order 5, 3, 2.

8) **arc** — Rearrange letters 1, 3, 5 in the order 5, 3, 1.

9) **hoe** — Rearrange letters 2, 3, 6 in the order 3, 2, 6.

10) **lag** — Rearrange letters 4, 6, 7 in the order 6, 7, 4.

11) **get** — Rearrange letters 2, 5, 8 in the order 8, 2, 5.

12) **end** — Rearrange letters 2, 3, 4 in the order 4, 2, 3.

13) **comet** — The first and last letters of the word move backward five places along the alphabet.

14) **oar** — Remove letters 2, 3, 4, 5, 6, 8 and 9, leaving the remaining letters in the order 1, 7, 10.

15) **rib** — Rearrange letters 5, 7, 8 in the order 7, 8, 5.

16) **wry** — Rearrange letters 2, 4, 9 in the order 4, 2, 9.

17) **hue** — Remove letters 3, 4, 5, 6, 7, 8 and 10, leaving the remaining letters in the order 1, 2, 9.

18) **ire** — Rearrange letters 3, 4, 10 in the order 3, 10, 4.

19) **rue** — Rearrange letters 3, 4, 6 in the order 3, 6, 4.

20) **nor** — Rearrange letters 6, 7, 10 in the order 7, 6, 10.

21) **caw** — Remove letters 3, 4, 6, 7, 8, 9 and 10, leaving the remaining letters in the order 1, 2, 5.

22) **wan** — Rearrange letters 1, 2, 7 in the order 7, 2, 1.

Section Two — Word Meanings

Page 16 — Closest Meaning

1) **ogle   gape** — Both of these mean 'to stare'.

2) **saturated   sodden** — Both of these mean 'wet through'.

3) **revive   resurrect** — Both of these mean 'to bring back to life'.

4) **sentinel   guard** — Both of these describe someone whose job is to watch over something.

5) **asset   benefit** — Both of these mean 'an aid'.

6) **impending   upcoming** — Both of these mean 'happening soon'.

7) **trounce   rout** — Both of these mean 'to defeat convincingly'.

8) **flummox   bewilder** — Both of these mean 'to confuse'.

9) **disclose   divulge** — Both of these mean 'to reveal a piece of information'.

10) **requisite   integral** — Both of these mean 'essential'.

11) **eclipse   surpass** — Both of these mean 'to outdo'.

12) **furnish   equip** — Both of these mean 'to provide someone with something'.

13) **astounded   flabbergasted** — Both of these mean 'shocked'.

14) **exacting   demanding** — Both of these mean 'requiring lots of effort or energy'.

15) **alias   pseudonym** — Both of these describe a false or assumed name.

16) **auxiliary   supplementary** — Both of these mean 'additional'.

17) **implicit   unspoken** — Both of these mean 'implied without being directly expressed'.

18) **florid   ornate** — Both of these mean 'elaborately decorated'.

19) **negligible   minor** — Both of these mean 'insignificant in amount'.

20) **compilation   anthology** — Both of these are collections of different pieces of writing.

Page 17 — Closest Meaning

1) **squalid   filthy** — Both of these mean 'extremely dirty'.

2) **obliging   accommodating** — Both of these mean 'eager to help'.

3) **pummel   bludgeon** — Both of these mean 'to strike forcefully'.

4) **efface   erase** — Both of these mean 'to delete'.

5) **stronghold   fortress** — Both of these mean 'a fortified place'.

6) **disconsolate   despondent** — Both of these mean 'very sad'.

7) **quibble   objection** — Both of these mean 'an issue'.

8) **opportune   timely** — Both of these mean 'at an ideal time'.

9) **sprightly   vivacious** — Both of these mean 'energetic'.

10) **brazen   impertinent** — Both of these mean 'bold, rude and shameless'.

11) **scoundrel   reprobate** — Both of these mean 'a person who behaves badly'.

12) **facetious   flippant** — Both of these mean 'treating serious issues lightly'.

13) **impactful   poignant** — Both of these mean 'deeply affecting'.

14) **provocative   inflammatory** — Both of these mean 'intended to arouse strong feelings'.

15) **petulant   irascible** — Both of these mean 'bad-tempered'.

16) **congenial   agreeable** — Both of these mean 'pleasant and amicable'.

17) **changeable   mercurial** — Both of these mean 'quick to change'.

18) **decorous   proper** — Both of these mean 'polite and respectable'.

19) **prodigal   thriftless** — Both of these mean 'wasteful'.

20) **pastoral   bucolic** — Both of these mean 'rural'.

Page 18 — Opposite Meaning

1) **unfurl   fold** — 'unfurl' means 'to unravel a piece of material', whereas 'fold' means 'to close a piece of material in on itself'.

2) **spindly   stocky** — 'spindly' means 'tall, thin and weak', whereas 'stocky' means 'short and sturdy'.

3) **phony   authentic** — 'phony' means 'fake', whereas 'authentic' means 'real'.

4) **hurtle   creep** — 'hurtle' means 'to move quickly and carelessly', whereas 'creep' means 'to move slowly and cautiously'.

5) **wasteful   frugal** — 'wasteful' means 'not careful with money', whereas 'frugal' means 'cautious about spending money'.

6) **jubilant   crestfallen** — 'jubilant' means 'very happy', whereas 'crestfallen' means 'very sad'.

7) **spurn   embrace** — 'spurn' means 'to reject', whereas 'embrace' means 'to willingly accept'.

8) **rigid   malleable** — 'rigid' means 'not able to bend easily', whereas 'malleable' means 'easy to bend'.

9) **dislodge   anchor** — 'dislodge' means 'to remove from a fixed position', whereas 'anchor' means 'to fix in place'.

10) **subdued   boisterous** — 'subdued' means 'quiet and calm', whereas 'boisterous' means 'loud and full of energy'.

11) **jeopardy   security** — 'jeopardy' means 'danger', whereas 'security' means 'safety'.

12) **prevalent   uncommon** — 'prevalent' means 'widespread', whereas 'uncommon' means 'rare'.

13) **daunt   hearten** — 'daunt' means 'to discourage', whereas 'hearten' means 'to encourage'.

14) **obscene   inoffensive** — 'obscene' means 'shocking and offensive', whereas 'inoffensive' means 'unlikely to cause offence'.

15) **assured   insecure** — 'assured' means 'comfortable and confident', whereas 'insecure' means 'lacking confidence'.

16) **ominous   encouraging** — 'ominous' means 'worrying', whereas 'encouraging' means 'promising'.

17) **proximity   remoteness** — 'proximity' means 'closeness', whereas 'remoteness' means 'distance'.

18) **cordiality   hostility** — 'cordiality' means 'friendliness', whereas 'hostility' means 'unfriendliness'.

19) **disgruntled   gratified** — 'disgruntled' means 'unsatisfied', whereas 'gratified' means 'satisfied'.

20) **vent   repress** — 'vent' means 'to let your emotions out', whereas 'repress' means 'to keep your emotions in'.

Page 19 — Opposite Meaning

1) **relinquish   withhold** — 'relinquish' means 'to give something up', whereas 'withhold' means 'to keep hold of something'.

2) **impulsive   calculated** — 'impulsive' means 'without thinking', whereas 'calculated' means 'carefully thought through'.

3) **integrity   deceitfulness** — 'integrity' means 'honesty', whereas 'deceitfulness' means 'dishonesty'.

4) **intuitive   learned** — 'intuitive' means 'based on impulse rather than instruction', whereas 'learned' means 'taken in through instruction'.

5) **remiss   attentive** — 'remiss' means 'not paying enough attention', whereas 'attentive' means 'careful to pay attention'.

6) **scrupulous   immoral** — 'scrupulous' means 'principled', whereas 'immoral' means 'unprincipled'.

7) **hollow   protrusion** — 'hollow' means 'an empty space in something', whereas 'protrusion' means 'an area that juts out of something'.

8) **compliant   wayward** — 'compliant' means 'willing to follow instructions', whereas 'wayward' means 'difficult to control'.

9) **destitute   opulent** — 'destitute' means 'extremely poor', whereas 'opulent' means 'very rich'.

10) **liberate   subjugate** — 'liberate' means 'to grant someone their freedom', whereas 'subjugate' means 'to forcefully bring someone under your control'.

11) **taboo   permissible** — 'taboo' means 'not accepted or discussed', whereas 'permissible' means 'accepted'.

12) **complimentary   defamatory** — 'complimentary' means 'approving', whereas 'defamatory' means 'strongly critical'.

13) **fortify   debilitate** — 'fortify' means 'strengthen', whereas 'debilitate' means 'weaken'.

14) **aberrant   typical** — 'aberrant' means 'abnormal', whereas 'typical' means 'normal'.

15) **incandescent   dim** — 'incandescent' means 'brightly lit', whereas 'dim' means 'not having much light'.

16) **expunge   preserve** — 'expunge' means 'to completely remove', whereas 'preserve' means 'to keep'.

17) **convoluted   direct** — 'convoluted' means 'complex', whereas 'direct' means 'clear'.

18) **abstemious   gluttonous** — 'abstemious' means 'moderate in behaviour', whereas 'gluttonous' means 'greedy'.

19) **belligerent   peaceable** — 'belligerent' means 'eager for a fight', whereas 'peaceable' means 'not wanting to fight'.

20) **loquacious   reticent** — 'loquacious' means 'talkative', whereas 'reticent' means 'reserved'.

Page 20 — Multiple Meanings

1) **legend** — 'legend' can mean 'a caption explaining a diagram' or 'a traditional and very old story'.

2) **curse** — 'curse' can mean 'magic words to bring someone misfortune' or 'to use impolite language'.

3) **launch** — 'launch' can mean 'to hurl through the air' or 'to begin'.

4) **crooked** — 'crooked' can mean 'not straight' or 'immoral'.

5) **shred** — 'shred' can mean 'to break into pieces' or 'a very small amount'.

6) **germ** — 'germ' can mean 'the beginning of something' or 'a tiny organism that causes disease'.

7) **fantastic** — 'fantastic' can mean 'excellent' or 'hard to believe'.

8) **scramble** — 'scramble' can mean 'to mix up' or 'to ascend'.

9) **diversion** — 'diversion' can mean 'a change from the original route' or 'an entertainment'.

10) **immediate** — 'immediate' can mean 'very close by' or 'without delay'.

11) **bother** — 'bother' can mean 'to irritate' or 'to go to the effort of doing something'.

12) **active** — 'active' can mean 'dynamic' or 'in operation'.

13) **grind** — 'grind' can mean 'to rub against a hard surface' or 'a monotonous, uninteresting activity'.

14) **implement** — 'implement' can mean 'an instrument' or 'to make something happen'.

15) **agitate** — 'agitate' can mean 'to mix around' or 'to distress'.

16) **pelt** — 'pelt' can mean 'an animal skin' or 'to throw with great force'.

17) **snag** — 'snag' can mean 'a problem' or 'to catch quickly'.

18) **repair** — 'repair' can mean 'to restore' or 'the state something is in'.

Page 21 — Multiple Meanings

1) **sustain** — 'sustain' can mean 'to experience something negative' or 'to keep'.

2) **slur** — 'slur' can mean 'an insult' or 'to speak incoherently'.

3) **lull** — 'lull' can mean 'a brief gap' or 'to calm'.

4) **trimming** — 'trimming' can mean 'a decoration' or 'cutting the edges off something'.

5) **blow** — 'blow' can mean 'to use all your money at once' or 'a disappointment'.

6) **shell** — 'shell' can mean 'to drop bombs on' or 'the outer layer of something'.

7) **raft** — 'raft' can mean 'a simple floating structure' or 'a large number'.

8) **groove** — 'groove' can mean 'a narrow indentation' or 'a familiar, fixed routine'.

9) **suspicion** — 'suspicion' can mean 'a tiny amount' or 'a feeling of mistrust'.

10) **dismiss** — 'dismiss' can mean 'to send away' or 'to write something off as unimportant'.

11) **contention** — 'contention' can mean 'an idea that you put forward' or 'a disagreement between two parties'.

12) **report** — 'report' can mean 'a loud noise' or 'a written record'.

13) **blast** — 'blast' can mean 'to criticise strongly' or 'a loud bang'.

14) **fleece** — 'fleece' can mean 'the wool of an animal' or 'to trick someone out of their money'.

15) **frisk** — 'frisk' can mean 'to move around energetically' or 'to search a person using your hands'.

16) **fuss** — 'fuss' can mean 'to pay great attention to someone in a doting way' or 'lots of noise and excitement'.

17) **dispatch** — 'dispatch' can mean 'to kill' or 'to send away quickly'.

18) **relieve** — 'relieve' can mean 'to make someone feel more at ease' or 'to take the place of someone doing a duty'.

19) **diminish** — 'diminish' can mean 'to become smaller' or 'to talk down about someone or something'.

20) **bounty** — 'bounty' can mean 'money paid as a reward' or 'willingness to give what you have'.

21) **moot** — 'moot' can mean 'to raise a point' or 'open to debate but without a definite answer'.

Page 22 — Odd Ones Out

1) **badge   label** — The other three are all used to attach things together.

2) **autobiography   thesaurus** — The other three are all publications that are released on a regular basis.

3) **trend   assessment** — The other three all mean 'prediction'.

4) **stool   bench** — The other three are all types of long, cushioned seats.

5) **folklore   anecdote** — The other three are all names for stories that teach a moral lesson.

6) **promote   advocate** — The other three all mean 'to take something in'.

7) **skirt   sleeve** — The other three all mean 'to cover up'.

8) **graze   collide** — The other three are all onomatopoeic words (words that sound like the sound they are describing).

9) **conviction   wish** — The other three all mean 'a feeling that something is going to happen'.

10) **sled   raft** — The other three all have wheels.

11) **dozen   batch** — The other three are all general words to describe a large group.

12) **forest   canyon** — The other three are all words to describe an open, flat area of grassland.

13) **armoury   ministry** — The other three are all branches of an army.

14) **frame   canvas** — The other three are all forms of artwork.

15) **ingest   absorb** — The other three all mean 'to give out'.

16) **bracelet   scarf** — The other three are all types of jewellery worn around the neck.

17) **current   procession** — The other three all mean 'a sudden rush or increase'.

18) **gland   rash** — The other three are all kinds of raised lumps that grow on the skin.

Page 23 — Odd Ones Out

1) **pair   duo** — The other three are all words to describe a group of more than two.

2) **sufficient   inadequate** — The other three all mean 'unnecessary'.

3) **lawn   conservatory** — The other three are all outdoor seating areas constructed next to a house.

4) **heroic   intrepid** — The other three all mean 'willing to take unnecessary risks'.

Answers

5) **indescribable unutterable** — The other three all mean 'impossible to comprehend'.

6) **spiritual ethereal** — The other three all mean 'ghost-like'.

7) **motif pattern** — The other three are all names for symbols used to identify someone or something.

8) **escapism exclusion** — The other three all mean 'the movement of people away from a place'.

9) **assembly conference** — The other three are all types of large, festive celebrations or spectacles.

10) **dialogue discussion** — The other three are all names for speeches given by a single person.

11) **witty apt** — The other three all mean 'short and to the point'.

12) **logical ingenious** — The other three all mean 'aware'.

13) **decanter pitcher** — The other three are all vessels that you drink from directly.

14) **tranquillity serenity** — The other three all mean 'polite behaviour'.

15) **brick slate** — The other three are all types of earth.

16) **critique review** — The other three all mean 'an angry speech criticising something'.

17) **paradox alliance** — The other three all describe something that corresponds to something else.

18) **supervisor merchant** — The other three are all words to describe a very influential and wealthy businessperson.

19) **compassion strategy** — The other three all mean 'care and caution'.

20) **sediment powder** — The other three all mean 'something with no or little value'.

21) **piece track** — The other three are all parts of a song.

22) **inherent expiring** — The other three all mean 'beginning to grow or develop'.

Page 24 — Word Connections

1) **hundred thousand** — They are the number of years in a century and a millennium.

2) **plentiful scanty** — They are synonyms of 'abundant' and 'scarce'.

3) **strain boil** — They are what a colander and a kettle are used for.

4) **sturdy infirm** — They are synonyms of 'robust' and 'feeble'.

5) **convene disperse** — They are synonyms of 'assemble' and 'disband'.

6) **tree flower** — They are what saplings and buds grow into.

7) **car tractor** — They are the vehicles that pull caravans and ploughs.

8) **powerful accomplished** — They are antonyms of 'impotent' and 'inept'.

9) **descendant heir** — They are synonyms of 'offspring' and 'successor'.

10) **condemn laud** — They are synonyms of 'deplore' and 'commend'.

11) **setback squabble** — They are less extreme versions of a fiasco and a feud.

12) **suspense amusement** — They are the feelings aroused by thrillers and comedies.

13) **forge kiln** — They are the types of ovens used for iron and pottery.

14) **legs tail** — They are body parts that snakes and humans do not have.

15) **mathematics science** — They are the subjects to which arithmetic and chemistry belong.

16) **police navy** — They are the organisations in which you would find an inspector and an admiral.

17) **phobia devotion** — They are extreme versions of uneasiness and fondness.

18) **salary pension** — They are the regular payments people typically receive when they are employed and retired.

19) **stumpy stout** — They are antonyms of 'lanky' and 'scrawny'.

20) **mine well** — They are where copper and oil are extracted.

Page 25 — Word Connections

1) **reimburse swindle** — They are synonyms of 'compensate' and 'cheat'.

2) **profound faithful** — They are antonyms of 'superficial' and 'fickle'.

3) **electricity flame** — They are what you use to illuminate a bulb and a candle.

4) **controversial established** — They are synonyms of 'contentious' and 'entrenched'.

5) **computer clock** — They are the inventions that made typewriters and sundials no longer necessary.

6) **composed easygoing** — They are antonyms of 'jittery' and 'testy'.

7) **cyclone quagmire** — They are alternative names for a hurricane and a bog.

8) **fishing construction** — They are the industries in which a trawler and a crane are used.

9) **inject spray** — They are the verbs used to describe what syringes and aerosols are used for.

10) **member participant** — They are the people who take part in societies and trials.

11) **invigorated idle** — They are antonyms of 'jaded' and 'industrious'.

12) **confiscate relinquish** — They are synonyms of 'commandeer' and 'waive'.

13) **violate conform** — They are synonyms of 'infringe' and 'obey'.

14) **harvest log** — They are the verbs used to describe the process of collecting crops and timber.

15) **lacklustre creative** — They are synonyms of 'uninspired' and 'innovative'.

16) **ancestry religion** — They are the topics that genealogy and theology focus on.

17) **marriage adulthood** — They are the points at which someone is no longer a bachelor and a child.

18) **city continent** — They are larger entities made up of districts and countries.

19) **government landlord** — They are the organisations or people who you pay tax and rent to.

20) **mountains sea** — They are the adjectives used to describe things relating to mountains or the sea.

Section Three — Maths and Sequences

Page 26 — Complete the Sum

1) **3** — $24 \div 3 + 12 - 8 = 12, 12 = 4 \times 3$

2) **13** — $6 \times 8 - 9 = 39, 39 = 15 \div 5 \times 13$

3) **16** — $7 \times 3 - 20 + 1 = 2, 2 = 16 \div 8$

4) **4** — $9 \times 7 - 14 + 3 = 52, 52 = 13 \times 4$

5) **9** — $35 \div 7 \times 9 - 18 = 27, 27 = 3 \times 9$

6) **12** — $56 \div 8 + 3 = 10, 10 = 21 - 12 + 1$

7) **10** — $6 \times 5 + 7 = 37, 37 = 10 \times 4 - 3$

8) **7** — $20 \div 4 \times 8 + 9 = 49, 49 = 7 \times 7$

9) **11** — $28 \div 4 \times 10 - 4 = 66, 66 = 6 \times 11$

10) **14** — $3 \times 12 \div 4 = 9, 9 = 18 + 5 - 14$

11) **9** — $45 \div 5 \times 7 + 9 = 72, 72 = 8 \times 9$

12) **15** — $12 \times 4 - 14 + 11 = 45, 45 = 3 \times 15$

13) **13** — $42 \div 7 + 17 = 23, 23 = 6 \times 6 - 13$

14) **7** — $18 \div 3 \times 11 + 18 = 84, 84 = 12 \times 7$

15) **15** — $5 \times 12 \div 6 - 7 = 3, 3 = 15 \div 5$

16) **11** — $32 \div 8 \times 12 - 4 = 44, 44 = 4 \times 11$

17) **10** — $30 \div 6 + 18 = 23, 23 = 41 - 10 - 8$

18) **17** — $60 \div 4 + 14 = 29, 29 = 43 - 17 + 3$

19) **4** — $6 \times 5 + 11 - 9 = 32, 32 = 41 - 13 + 4$

20) **7** — $8 \times 3 - 7 + 15 = 32, 32 = 6 \times 7 - 10$

Page 27 — Complete the Sum

1) **18** — $48 \div 12 + 7 - 5 = 6, 6 = 3 \times 8 - 18$

2) **7** — $6 \times 9 - 16 + 4 = 42, 42 = 7 \times 5 + 7$

3) **3** — $8 \times 5 \div 4 + 13 = 23, 23 = 36 \div 3 + 11$

4) **27** — $26 \div 2 - 7 + 21 = 27, 27 = 6 \times 9 - 27$

5) **33** — $11 \times 5 + 17 - 24 = 48, 48 = 33 - 14 + 29$

6) **13** — $5 \times 7 - 27 + 11 = 19, 19 = 30 \div 5 + 13$

7) **7** — $72 \div 6 - 9 + 18 = 21, 21 = 7 \times 4 - 7$

Answers

8) **11** — 12 × 4 − 16 + 29 = 61, 61 = 9 × 8 − 11
9) **3** — 81 ÷ 9 + 13 − 17 = 5, 5 = 3 × 7 − 16
10) **60** — 6 × 6 ÷ 12 + 8 = 11, 11 = 48 − 60 + 23
11) **15** — 88 ÷ 11 − 3 + 17 = 22, 22 = 42 ÷ 6 + 15
12) **10** — 10 × 9 + 23 − 75 = 38, 38 = 10 × 6 − 22
13) **8** — 12 × 7 + 67 − 95 = 56, 56 = 28 ÷ 4 × 8
14) **4** — 64 ÷ 8 × 12 + 25 = 121, 121 = 44 ÷ 4 × 11
15) **24** — 11 × 12 + 29 − 83 − 18 = 60, 60 = 9 × 4 + 24
16) **23** — 12 × 10 ÷ 8 + 43 − 21 = 37, 37 = 12 × 5 − 23
17) **15** — 12 × 7 ÷ 6 + 17 − 9 = 22, 22 = 56 ÷ 8 + 15
18) **7** — 120 ÷ 12 × 4 − 37 + 45 = 48, 48 = 7 × 12 − 36
19) **9** — 121 ÷ 11 × 9 + 9 − 59 = 49, 49 = 63 ÷ 9 × 7
20) **8** — 9 × 11 ÷ 3 + 18 − 23 = 28, 28 = 12 × 3 − 8
21) **7** — 72 ÷ 9 × 12 − 19 − 38 = 39, 39 = 21 ÷ 7 × 13
22) **12** — 144 ÷ 12 × 11 − 37 − 19 = 76, 76 = 12 × 8 − 20

Page 28 — Letter Sequences

1) **QV** — The first letter in each pair moves in the sequence -1, -2, -3, -4, -5. The second letter in each pair moves forward 2 letters each time.
2) **RY** — The first letter in the pair moves in the sequence +5, +3, +1, -1, -3. The second letter moves forward 4 letters each time.
3) **KF** — The first letter in each pair moves back 2 letters and then back 1 letter alternately. The second letter in each pair moves in the sequence +3, +4, +5, +6, +7.
4) **BM** — The first letter in each pair moves forward 2 letters each time. The second letter in each pair moves in the sequence -3, -4, -5, -6, -7.
5) **AW** — The first letter in each pair moves in the sequence +5, +4, +3, +2, +1. The second letter in each pair moves forward 1 letter and then forward 5 letters alternately.
6) **EA** — The first letter in each pair moves back 1 letter and then forward 5 letters alternately. The second letter in each pair moves in the sequence +3, +5, +7, +9, +11.
7) **XY** — The first letter in each pair moves in the sequence +4, +6, +8, +10, +12. The second letter in each pair moves forward 2 letters and then forward 1 letter alternately.
8) **PF** — The first letter in each pair moves forward 4 letters and then back 3 letters alternately. The second letter in each pair moves in the sequence +1, +3, +5, +7, +9.
9) **RN** — The first letter in each pair moves forward 3 letters and then back 5 letters alternately. The second letter in each pair moves in the sequence -4, -5, -6, -7, -8.
10) **AZ** — The first letter in each pair moves in the sequence -1, -3, -5, -7, -9. The second letter in each pair moves back 5 letters and then back 2 letters alternately.
11) **UR** — The first letter in each pair moves in the sequence +2, +4, +6, +8, +10. The second letter in each pair moves forward 1 letter and then forward 4 letters alternately.
12) **LE** — The first letter in each pair moves back 4 letters and then back 5 letters alternately. The second letter in each pair moves in the sequence +5, +4, +3, +2, +1.
13) **WF** — The first letter in each pair moves forward 5 letters and then back 3 letters alternately. The second letter in each pair moves in the sequence -3, -4, -5, -6, -7.
14) **GS** — The first letter in each pair moves back 4 letters and then back 1 letter alternately. The second letter in each pair moves in the sequence +1, +3, +5, +7, +9.
15) **HR** — The first letter in each pair moves forward 3 letters and then forward 5 letters alternately. The second letter in each pair moves in the sequence +3, +2, +1, 0, -1.
16) **YF** — The first letter in each pair moves in the sequence -2, -4, -6, -8, -10. The second letter in each pair moves forward 1 letter and then forward 3 letters alternately.
17) **XR** — The first letter in each pair moves back 2 letters and then forward 5 letters alternately. The second letter in each pair moves in the sequence +1, +3, +5, +7, +9.
18) **ZI** — The first letter in each pair moves in the sequence +4, +6, +8, +10, +12. The second letter in each pair moves back 2 letters and then forward 3 letters alternately.

19) **HB** — The first letter in each pair moves in the sequence -5, -6, -7, -8, -9. The second letter in each pair moves forward 2 letters and then forward 4 letters alternately.
20) **IY** — The first letter in each pair moves in the sequence +1, 0, -1, -2, -3. The second letter in each pair moves back 4 letters and then back 1 letter alternately.

Page 29 — Letter Sequences

1) **XP** — The first letter in each pair moves back 4 letters and then back 1 letter alternately. The second letter in each pair moves in the sequence +3, +5, +7, +9, +11.
2) **DG** — The first letter in the pair moves back 3 letters and then back 2 letters alternately. The second letter moves in the sequence -4, -3, -2, -1, 0.
3) **OK** — The first letter in each pair moves in the sequence +4, +6, +8, +10, +12. The second letter in each pair moves forward 3 letters and then forward 2 letters alternately.
4) **SF** — The first letter in each pair moves back 3 letters and then back 1 letter alternately. The second letter in each pair moves in the sequence -5, -7, -9, -11, -13.
5) **VT** — The first letter in each pair moves in the sequence -2, -1, 0, +1, +2. The second letter in each pair moves back 2 letters and then back 3 letters alternately.
6) **ZT** — The first letter in each pair moves in the sequence +4, +3, +2, +1, 0. The second letter in each pair moves back 3 letters and then back 4 letters alternately.
7) **IP** — The first letter in each pair moves in the sequence -5, -7, -9, -11, -13. The second letter in each pair moves forward 5 letters and then back 2 letters alternately.
8) **IU** — The first letter in each pair moves in the sequence -3, -1, +1, +3, +5. The second letter in each pair moves forward 3 letters and then forward 4 letters alternately.
9) **VR** — The first letter in each pair moves back 4 letters and then back 1 letter alternately. The second letter in each pair moves in the sequence +3, +5, +7, +9, +11.
10) **HD** — The first letter in each pair moves back 2 letters and then back 3 letters alternately. The second letter in each pair moves in the sequence -3, -4, -5, -6, -7.
11) **ZM** — The first letter in each pair moves back 4 letters and then forward 3 letters alternately. The second letter in each pair moves in the sequence +5, +3, +1, -1, -3.
12) **CF** — The first letter in each pair moves in the sequence -4, -6, -8, -10, -12. The second letter in each pair moves forward 3 letters and then forward 2 letters alternately.
13) **UL** — The first letter in each pair moves forward 2 letters and then forward 4 letters alternately. The second letter in each pair moves in the sequence -4, -6, -8, -10, -12.
14) **PL** — The first letter in the pair moves forward 3 letters and then back 5 letters alternately. The second letter moves in the sequence -5, -3, -1, +1, +3.
15) **KE** — The first letter in the pair moves in the sequence -9, -6, -3, 0, +3 (the number added increases by 3 each time). The second letter moves in the sequence +16, +8, +4, +2, +1 (the number added halves each time).
16) **DD** — The first letter in the pair moves forward 8 letters and then back 3 letters alternately. The second letter moves in the sequence -5, 0, +5, +10, +15 (the number added increases by 5 each time).
17) **BX** — The first letter in the pair moves back 9 letters and then forward 5 letters alternately. The second letter moves in the sequence +4, +8, +12, +16, +20 (the number added increases by 4 each time).
18) **VT** — The first letter in the pair moves in the sequence -6, -1, +4, +9, +14 (the number added increases by 5 each time). The second letter moves back 11 letters and then forward 7 letters alternately.
19) **DM** — The first letter in the pair moves in the sequence +11, +13, +15, +17, +19, +21. The second letter moves back 3 letters, then forward 2 letters, and then back 4 letters alternately.
20) **GU** — The first letter in the pair moves forward 4 letters, then forward 5 letters, and then back 6 letters alternately. The second letter moves in the sequence +2, -2, -6, -10, -14, -18 (the number added decreases by 4 each time).

Answers

21) HI — The first letter in the sequence moves forward 5 letters, then forward 7 letters, and then forward 11 letters alternately. The second letter in the pair moves in the sequence +1, +6, +11, +16, +21, +26 (the number added increases by 5 each time).

22) SO — The first letter in the pair moves forward 8 letters, then back 3 letters, and then back 10 letters alternately. The second letter moves in the sequence -8, -5, -2, +1, +4, +7 (the number added increases by 3 each time).

Page 30 — Number Sequences

1) **57** — The two previous numbers are added together to get the next number in the sequence.

2) **39** — Subtract odd numbers in ascending order: -1, -3, -5, -7, -9.

3) **33** — Add prime numbers in ascending order: +2, +3, +5, +7, +11.

4) **24** — There are two sequences which alternate. In the first sequence, the number doubles each time. In the second sequence, the number halves each time.

5) **22** — Subtract square numbers in descending order: -25, -16, -9, -4, -1.

6) **98** — The number added halves each time: +48, +24, +12, +6, +3.

7) **8** — There are two sequences which alternate. In both sequences, the number doubles each time.

8) **67** — Add odd numbers in descending order: +17, +15, +13, +11, +9.

9) **5** — Subtract even numbers in ascending order: -4, -6, -8, -10, -12.

10) **11** — Subtract prime numbers in ascending order: -5, -7, -11, -13, -17.

11) **137** — The two previous numbers are added together to get the next number in the sequence.

12) **76** — The number subtracted halves each time: -64, -32, -16, -8, -4.

13) **128** — There are two sequences which alternate. In both sequences, the number is multiplied by 4 each time.

14) **62** — Add square numbers in descending order: +25, +16, +9, +4, +1.

15) **129** — The number added doubles each time: +1, +2, +4, +8, +16.

16) **34** — Add prime numbers in descending order: +11, +7, +5, +3, +2.

17) **10** — There are two sequences which alternate. In the first sequence, the number halves each time. In the second sequence, the number doubles each time.

18) **5** — Subtract even numbers in ascending order: -16, -14, -12, -10, -8.

19) **36** — The numbers follow the sequence -5, 0, +5, +10, +15 (the number added increases by 5 each time).

20) **48** — Multiply by ascending numbers: ×1, ×2, ×3, ×4.

Page 31 — Number Sequences

1) **113** — Add odd numbers in ascending order: +3, +5, +7, +9, +11.

2) **22** — Subtract prime numbers in descending order: -11, -7, -5, -3, -2.

3) **183** — The numbers follow the sequence -14, 0, +14, +28, +42.

4) **27** — There are two sequences which alternate. In the first sequence, the numbers are multiplied by 3 each time. In the second sequence, add 11 each time.

5) **1** — Divide by ascending numbers: ÷2, ÷3, ÷4, ÷5.

6) **0** — Subtract square numbers in ascending order: -1, -4, -9, -16, -25.

7) **133** — Add even numbers in ascending order: +6, +8, +10, +12, +14.

8) **66** — Subtract odd numbers in descending order: -13, -11, -9, -7, -5.

9) **93** — Add square numbers in ascending order: +4, +9, +16, +25, +36.

10) **24** — There are two sequences which alternate. In the first sequence, subtract 3 each time. In the second sequence, multiply by 3 each time.

11) **360** — Multiply by descending numbers: ×5, ×4, ×3, ×2.

12) **2** — There are two sequences which alternate. In the first sequence, the number is divided by 3 each time. In the second sequence, the number is multiplied by 3 each time.

13) **16** — There are two sequences which alternate. In the first sequence, subtract 8 each time. In the second sequence, the number is divided by 4 each time.

14) **2** — Divide by descending numbers: ÷5, ÷4, ÷3, ÷2.

15) **120** — The numbers follow the sequence +27, +18, +9, 0, -9.

16) **4** — Divide by descending prime numbers: ÷11, ÷7, ÷5, ÷3.

17) **12** — There are two sequences which alternate. In the first sequence, add odd numbers in ascending order: +1, +3, +5. In the second sequence, subtract even numbers in descending order: -6, -4.

18) **69** — The numbers follow the sequence: +1, -1, -3, -5, -7.

19) **1** — Divide by descending odd numbers: ÷9, ÷7, ÷5, ÷3, ÷1.

20) **32** — The two previous numbers are multiplied together to get the next number in the sequence.

21) **125** — These are cube numbers, i.e. 1 × 1 × 1 = 1, 2 × 2 × 2 = 8, 3 × 3 × 3 = 27 etc.

22) **105** — There are two sequences which alternate. In the first sequence, the number is multiplied by descending odd numbers: ×7, ×5, ×3. In the second sequence, add descending square numbers: +9, +4.

Page 32 — Related Numbers

1) **24** — Add the two outer numbers together (5 + 7 = 12). Multiply the answer by 2 (12 × 2 = 24).

2) **1** — Multiply the two outer numbers (1 × 5 = 5). Divide the answer by 5 (5 ÷ 5 = 1).

3) **27** — Add the two outer numbers together (5 + 4 = 9). Multiply the answer by 3 (9 × 3 = 27).

4) **7** — Divide the third number by the first number (36 ÷ 12 = 3). Add 4 to the answer (3 + 4 = 7).

5) **15** — Double the third number (11 × 2 = 22). Subtract the first number from the answer (22 − 7 = 15).

6) **7** — Subtract the first number from the third (23 − 2 = 21). Divide the answer by 3 (21 ÷ 3 = 7).

7) **18** — Multiply the two outer numbers (6 × 9 = 54). Divide the answer by 3 (54 ÷ 3 = 18).

8) **12** — Divide the first number by the third number (48 ÷ 8 = 6). Multiply the answer by 2 (6 × 2 = 12).

9) **3** — Add the two outer numbers together (3 + 6 = 9). Divide the answer by 3 (9 ÷ 3 = 3).

10) **6** — Add 5 to the third number (37 + 5 = 42). Divide the answer by the first number (42 ÷ 7 = 6).

11) **16** — Divide the third number by the first (64 ÷ 8 = 8). Add the answer to the first number (8 + 8 = 16).

12) **25** — Add the two outer numbers together (3 + 2 = 5). Square the answer (5 × 5 = 25).

13) **10** — Divide the third number by the first (20 ÷ 4 = 5). Add 5 (5 + 5 = 10).

14) **18** — Find the mid-point of the two outer numbers by adding them together and dividing the answer by 2 (12 + 22 = 34) (34 ÷ 2 = 17). Add 1 (17 + 1 = 18).

15) **31** — Add the two outer numbers together (1 + 10 = 11). Multiply the answer by 3 (11 × 3 = 33). Subtract 2 (33 − 2 = 31).

16) **14** — Multiply the two outer numbers (9 × 3 = 27). Add 1 (27 + 1 = 28). Divide by 2 (28 ÷ 2 = 14).

17) **16** — Find the mid-point of the two outer numbers (10 + 12 = 22) (22 ÷ 2 = 11). Add 5 (11 + 5 = 16).

18) **9** — Subtract the first number from the third (33 − 17 = 16). Divide the answer by 2 (16 ÷ 2 = 8). Add 1 (8 + 1 = 9).

19) **12** — Find the mid-point of the two outer numbers (2 + 6 = 8) (8 ÷ 2 = 4). Multiply the answer by 3 (4 × 3 = 12).

20) **16** — Subtract the third number from the first (36 − 6 = 30). Divide the answer by 3 (30 ÷ 3 = 10). Add 6 (10 + 6 = 16).

Page 33 — Related Numbers

1) **19** — Find the mid-point of the two outer numbers (14 + 18 = 32) (32 ÷ 2 = 16). Add 3 (16 + 3 = 19).

2) **31** — Multiply the two outer numbers (6 × 9 = 54). Halve the answer (54 ÷ 2 = 27). Add 4 (27 + 4 = 31).

3) **63** — Divide the first number by the third (21 ÷ 3 = 7). Add 2 (7 + 2 = 9). Multiply the answer by 7 (9 × 7 = 63).

4) **22** — Subtract the third number from the first (16 − 9 = 7). Multiply by 3 (7 × 3 = 21). Add 1 (21 + 1 = 22).

5) **64** — Add the outer numbers together (6 + 10 = 16). Then multiply the answer by 4 (16 × 4 = 64).

6) **36** — Divide the third number by the first ($55 \div 5 = 11$). Multiply by 3 ($11 \times 3 = 33$). Add 3 ($33 + 3 = 36$).

7) **48** — Subtract the third number from the first ($20 - 4 = 16$). Then multiply the answer by 3 ($16 \times 3 = 48$).

8) **16** — Find the mid-point of the two outer numbers ($5 + 15 = 20$) ($20 \div 2 = 10$). Subtract 2 ($10 - 2 = 8$). Multiply the answer by 2 ($8 \times 2 = 16$).

9) **24** — Multiply the two outer numbers ($13 \times 4 = 52$). Halve the answer ($52 \div 2 = 26$). Subtract 2 ($26 - 2 = 24$).

10) **13** — Square the first number ($1 \times 1 = 1$). Add the two outer numbers together ($1 + 13 = 14$). Subtract 1 ($14 - 1 = 13$).

11) **18** — Subtract the first number from the third ($71 - 37 = 34$). Divide by 2 ($34 \div 2 = 17$). Add 1 ($17 + 1 = 18$).

12) **16** — Square the two outer numbers ($2 \times 2 = 4$) ($8 \times 8 = 64$). Divide the third number by the first number ($64 \div 4 = 16$).

13) **10** — Divide the first number by 2 ($16 \div 2 = 8$). Add the answer to the third number ($8 + 1 = 9$). Add 1 ($9 + 1 = 10$).

14) **19** — Divide the third number by the first ($10 \div 1 = 10$). Multiply by 2 ($10 \times 2 = 20$). Subtract 1 ($20 - 1 = 19$).

15) **71** — Multiply the two outer numbers ($7 \times 9 = 63$). Add the first number to the answer ($7 + 63 = 70$). Add 1 ($70 + 1 = 71$).

16) **64** — Add the two outer numbers together ($5 + 3 = 8$). Square the answer ($8 \times 8 = 64$).

17) **14** — Multiply the two outer numbers ($4 \times 6 = 24$). Add the answer to the first number ($24 + 4 = 28$). Halve the answer ($28 \div 2 = 14$).

18) **2** — Subtract the first number from the third ($9 - 7 = 2$). Divide the answer by 2 ($2 \div 2 = 1$). Add 1 ($1 + 1 = 2$).

19) **29** — Square the two outer numbers ($3 \times 3 = 9$, $7 \times 7 = 49$). Then find their midpoint ($9 + 49 = 58$, $58 \div 2 = 29$).

20) **74** — Multiply the two outer numbers ($3 \times 8 = 24$). Multiply the answer by the first number ($24 \times 3 = 72$). Add 2 ($72 + 2 = 74$).

21) **11** — Multiply the third number by 4 ($2 \times 4 = 8$). Add the answer to the first number ($8 + 14 = 22$). Halve the answer ($22 \div 2 = 11$).

22) **15** — Add the two outer numbers together ($8 + 2 = 10$). Multiply the answer by the third number ($10 \times 2 = 20$). Subtract 5 ($20 - 5 = 15$).

Page 34 — Letter-Coded Sums

1) **E** — $6 + 23 + 11 - 17 = 23$, E = 23
2) **B** — $8 \times 6 - 34 - 8 = 6$, B = 6
3) **E** — $12 \times 5 - 27 - 5 = 28$, E = 28
4) **A** — $38 \div 19 + 25 - 16 = 11$, A = 11
5) **C** — $44 \div 22 + 9 + 10 = 21$, C = 21
6) **D** — $28 \div 7 \times 9 - 11 = 25$, D = 25
7) **B** — $36 \div 12 + 38 - 22 = 19$, B = 19
8) **C** — $24 \div 8 + 26 - 7 = 22$, C = 22
9) **E** — $40 \times 2 - 28 - 12 = 40$, E = 40
10) **B** — $36 \div 9 + 32 - 27 = 9$, B = 9
11) **E** — $18 \div 9 \times 15 + 9 = 39$, E = 39
12) **B** — $33 \div 11 + 26 - 11 = 18$, B = 18
13) **C** — $28 \div 7 + 25 - 12 = 17$, C = 17
14) **E** — $6 \times 12 \div 9 + 5 = 13$, E = 13
15) **A** — $12 \times 8 - 45 - 43 = 8$, A = 8
16) **E** — $16 \times 6 \div 12 + 24 = 32$, E = 32

Page 35 — Letter-Coded Sums

1) **C** — $27 \div 3 + 16 - 7 - 3 = 15$, C = 15
2) **B** — $10 \times 4 \div 8 + 26 - 23 = 8$, B = 8
3) **D** — $18 \div 6 + 22 - 15 + 8 = 18$, D = 18
4) **A** — $22 \div 11 + 29 - 13 - 9 = 9$, A = 9
5) **D** — $28 \div 7 \times 9 + 17 - 28 = 25$, D = 25
6) **E** — $8 \div 4 \times 12 + 20 - 12 = 32$, E = 32
7) **E** — $16 \div 4 \times 9 - 16 + 8 = 28$, E = 28

8) **E** — $11 \times 6 \div 3 + 14 - 18 = 18$, E = 18
9) **B** — $15 \div 5 + 22 - 5 - 10 = 10$, B = 10
10) **D** — $45 \div 9 \times 12 \div 4 + 9 = 24$, D = 24
11) **C** — $50 \div 5 \times 9 - 29 - 32 = 29$, C = 29
12) **B** — $13 \times 5 - 30 + 5 - 33 = 7$, B = 7
13) **B** — $11 \times 13 - 59 - 60 - 11 = 13$, B = 13
14) **A** — $8 \times 12 \div 16 \times 4 - 12 - 8 = 4$, A = 4
15) **B** — $12 \div 2 \times 3 \times 5 \div 15 - 3 = 3$, B = 3
16) **D** — $6 \times 8 \div 16 \times 21 \div 9 + 9 = 16$, D = 16
17) **B** — $66 \div 6 \times 12 \div 6 - 18 + 6 = 10$, B = 10
18) **C** — $36 \times 3 \div 9 + 81 - 63 + 3 + 3 = 36$, C = 36

Section Four — Logic and Coding

Page 36 — Letter Connections

1) **PL** — The first letter in the pair moves back 4 letters, the second letter moves back 6 letters.

2) **IF** — The first letter in the pair moves forward 7 letters, the second letter moves forward 3 letters.

3) **ET** — The first letter in the pair moves back 5 letters, the second letter moves back 8 letters.

4) **XR** — KP and EV are mirror pairs, where the two letters are an equal distance from the centre of the alphabet. The answer will be the mirror pairs for I and C, which are R and X, but the letters are reversed.

5) **SW** — The first letter in the pair moves forward 7 letters, the second letter moves back 5 letters.

6) **DW** — HS, JQ and BY are mirror pairs, where the two letters are an equal distance from the centre of the alphabet. J is 2 letters forward from H, so the missing mirror pair is DW, because D is 2 letters forward from B, and W is its mirror pair.

7) **TU** — The letters in the pair move back 9 letters.

8) **NF** — The first letter in the pair moves back 8 letters, the second letter moves forward 6 letters.

9) **MO** — The first letter in the pair moves forward 6 letters, the second letter moves back 7 letters.

10) **LO** — AZ, FU and GT are mirror pairs, where the two letters are an equal distance from the centre of the alphabet. F is 5 letters forward from A, so the missing mirror pair is LO, because L is 5 letters forward from G, and O is its mirror pair.

11) **EV** — NM, IR and JQ are mirror pairs, where the two letters are an equal distance from the centre of the alphabet. I is 5 letters back from N, so the missing mirror pair is EV, because E is five letters back from J, and V is its mirror pair.

12) **DU** — The first letter in the pair moves forward 7 letters, the second letter moves back 5 letters.

13) **KO** — The first letter in the pair moves back 8 letters, the second letter moves forward 4 letters.

14) **MF** — DW and JQ are mirror pairs, where the two letters are an equal distance from the centre of the alphabet. The answer will be the mirror pairs for U and N, which are F and M, but the letters are reversed.

15) **ZA** — BY, VE and FU are mirror pairs, where the two letters are an equal distance from the centre of the alphabet. V is 6 letters back from B, so the missing mirror pair is ZA, because Z is 6 letters back from F, and A is its mirror pair.

16) **ZT** — The first letter in the pair moves forward 9 letters, the second letter moves back 10 letters.

17) **CY** — The first letter in the pair moves back 4 letters, the second letter moves forward 5 letters.

18) **MN** — GT, KP and IR are mirror pairs, where the two letters are an equal distance from the centre of the alphabet. K is 4 letters forward from G, so the missing mirror pair is MN, because M is 4 letters forward from I, and N is its mirror pair.

19) **JK** — The first letter in the pair moves forward 11 letters, the second letter moves forward 2 letters.

20) **FU** — LO, SH and YB are mirror pairs, where the two letters are an equal distance from the centre of the alphabet. S is 7 letters forward from L, so the missing mirror pair is FU, because F is 7 letters forward from Y, and U is its mirror pair.

Page 37 — Letter Connections

1) **RZ** — The first letter in the pair moves back 12 letters, the second letter moves back 4 letters.

2) **AX** — JQ and HS are mirror pairs, where the two letters are an equal distance from the centre of the alphabet. The answer will be the mirror pairs for C and Z, which are X and A, but the letters are reversed.

3) **KX** — The first letter in the pair moves forward 7 letters, the second letter moves back 12 letters.

4) **LF** — The first letter in the pair moves back 9 letters, the second letter moves forward 10 letters.

5) **HH** — The first letter in the pair moves back 8 letters, the second letter moves back 12 letters.

6) **WD** — BY, RI and GT are mirror pairs, where the two letters are an equal distance from the centre of the alphabet. R is 10 letters back from B, so the missing mirror pair is WD, because W is 10 letters back from G, and D is its mirror pair.

7) **RI** — ZA, UF and WD are mirror pairs, where the two letters are an equal distance from the centre of the alphabet. U is 5 letters back from Z, so the missing mirror pair is RI because R is 5 letters back from W, and I is its mirror pair.

8) **JN** — The first letter in the pair moves back 6 letters, the second letter moves back 7 letters.

9) **ZO** — The first letter in the pair moves back 8 letters, the second letter moves forward 6 letters.

10) **YE** — The first letter in the pair moves forward 5 letters, the second letter moves forward 8 letters.

11) **KB** — NM and VE are mirror pairs, where the two letters are an equal distance from the centre of the alphabet. The answer will be the mirror pairs for Y and P, which are B and K, but the letters are reversed.

12) **IR** — KP, QJ and CX are mirror pairs, where the two letters are an equal distance from the centre of the alphabet. Q is 6 letters forward from K, so the missing mirror pair is IR, because I is 6 letters forward from C, and R is its mirror pair.

13) **RK** — The first letter in the pair moves forward 9 letters, the second letter moves back 5 letters.

14) **KP** — UF, BY and DW are mirror pairs, where the two letters are an equal distance from the centre of the alphabet. B is 7 letters forward from U, so the missing mirror pair is KP, because K is 7 letters forward from D, and P is its mirror pair.

15) **VE** — ZA, SH and CX are mirror pairs, where the two letters are an equal distance from the centre of the alphabet. S is 7 letters back from Z, so the missing mirror pair is VE, because V is 7 letters back from C, and E is its mirror pair.

16) **ER** — The first letter in the pair moves back 7 letters, the second letter moves forward 6 letters.

17) **MV** — The first letter in the pair moves forward 7 letters, the second letter moves forward 1 letter.

18) **UK** — The first letter in the pair moves forward 12 letters, the second letter moves forward 13 letters.

19) **LQ** — The first letter in the pair moves forward 10 letters, the second letter moves back 10 letters.

20) **SV** — The first letter in the pair moves back 12 letters, the second letter moves forward 8 letters.

21) **QN** — The first letter in the pair moves back 12 letters, the second letter moves forward 11 letters.

22) **JQ** — VE, MN and SH are mirror pairs, where the two letters are an equal distance from the centre of the alphabet. M is 9 letters back from V, so the missing mirror pair is JQ because J is 9 letters back from S, and Q is its mirror pair.

Page 38 — Letter-Word Codes

1) **IQNF** — To get from the word to the code move each letter forward 2.

2) **KIND** — To get from the code to the word move each letter forward 3.

3) **OHEL** — To get from the word to the code move each letter back 4.

4) **CREW** — This is a mirror code, where each letter is an equal distance from the centre of the alphabet. X is 11 letters forward from the centre, and C is 11 letters back; I is 5 letters back and R is 5 letters forward; V is 9 letter forwards and E is 9 letters back; D is 10 letters back and W is 10 letters forward.

5) **RKKG** — To get from the word to the code move the letters in the sequence −2, +2, −2, +2.

6) **XIPS** — To get from the word to the code move the letters in the sequence −2, +4, −2, +4.

7) **HER** — To get from the code to the word move the letters in the sequence +1, +2, +3.

8) **RANT** — This is a mirror code, where each letter is an equal distance from the centre of the alphabet. I is 5 letters back from the centre, and R is 5 letters forward; Z is 13 letters forward and A is 13 letters back; M is 1 letter back and N is 1 letter forward; G is 7 letters back and T is 7 letters forward.

9) **WTMCX** — To get from the word to the code move the letters in the sequence +4, −3, +4, −3, +4.

10) **YUMMY** — To get from the code to the word move the letters in the sequence −1, −2, −3, −4, −5.

11) **BLUSH** — To get from the code to the word move the letters in the sequence −3, −2, −1, 0, +1.

12) **YLZDM** — To get from the word to the code move the letters in the sequence +5, −3, +5, −3, +5.

13) **DQYPC** — To get from the word to the code move the letters in the sequence −2, +5, −2, +5, −2.

14) **CHEST** — To get from the code to the word move the letters in the sequence −1, −2, −3, −4, −5.

15) **SLIME** — This is a mirror code, where each letter is an equal distance from the centre of the alphabet. H is 6 letters back from the centre, and S is 6 letters forward; O is 2 letters forward and L is 2 letters back; R is 5 letters forward and I is 5 letters back; N is 1 letter forward and M is 1 letter back; V is 9 letters forward and E is 9 letters back.

Page 39 — Letter-Word Codes

1) **QLXBS** — To get from the word to the code move the letters in the sequence +1, −3, +1, −3, +1.

2) **NPVRO** — To get from the word to the code move the letters in the sequence −5, +4, −5, +4, −5.

3) **POUCH** — To get from the code to the word move the letters in the sequence +2, +4, +6, +4, +2.

4) **CNDMQ** — To get from the word to the code move the letters in the sequence −3, +5, −3, +5, −3.

5) **GLAD** — To get from the code to the word move the letters in the sequence +3, +4, +3, +4.

6) **BLANK** — To get from the code to the word move the letters in the sequence −2, +4, −2, +4, −2.

7) **MLEVO** — This is a mirror code, where each letter is an equal distance from the centre of the alphabet. N is 1 letter forward from the centre, and M is 1 letter back; O is 2 letters forward and L is 2 letters back; V is 9 letters forward and E is 9 letters back.

8) **FLASH** — To get from the code to the word move the letters in the sequence −2, −1, 0, +1 +2.

9) **DPEHC** — To get from the word to the code move the letters in the sequence 0, −2, −4, −6, −8.

10) **DAISY** — To get from the code to the word move the letters in the sequence −2, −4, −6, −8, −10.

11) **MORE** — To get from the code to the word move the letters in the sequence +2, −5, +2, −5.

12) **AITUH** — To get from the word to the code move the letters in the sequence −5, −3 −1, +1, +3.

13) **VDAJS** — To get from the word to the code move the letters in the sequence −3, +3, −2, +2 −1.

14) **STYLE** — To get from the code to the word move the letters in the sequence −1, +2, −3, +4, −5.

15) **LQNSJS** — To get from the word to the code move the letters in the sequence −1, +2, 0, −1, +2, 0.

16) **CHAOS** — To get from the code to the word move the letters in the sequence 0, −2, +4, −6, +8.

17) **RNNFDR** — To get from the word to the code move the letters in the sequence +2, −1, 0, +2, −1, 0.

18) **LAPSE** — To get from the code to the word move the letters in the sequence −1, +3, −5, +7, −9.

19) **QROLJK** — To get from the word to the code move the letters in the sequence −2, +2, −3, +3, −4, +4.

Answers

Page 40 — Number-Word Codes

1) **4532** — W = 4, O = 5, V = 3, E = 2
2) **3216** — V = 3, E = 2, I = 1, L = 6
3) **LOVE** — L = 6, O = 5, V = 3, E = 2
4) **5416** — R = 5, A = 4, C = 1, E = 6
5) **2514** — O = 2, R = 5, C = 1, A = 4
6) **MARE** — M = 3, A = 4, R = 5, E = 6
7) **1562** — F = 1, A = 5, C = 6, T = 2
8) **6513** — C = 6, A = 5, F = 1, E = 3
9) **HEFT** — H = 4, E = 3, F = 1, T = 2
10) **3156** — S = 3, O = 1, R = 5, E = 6
11) **2163** — T = 2, O = 1, E = 6, S = 3
12) **REST** — R = 5, E = 6, S = 3, T = 2

Page 41 — Number-Word Codes

1) **2341** — U = 2, N = 3, I = 4, T = 1
2) **1263** — T = 1, U = 2, R = 6, N = 3
3) **MINT** — M = 5, I = 4, N = 3, T = 1
4) **6524** — C = 6, L = 5, A = 2, D = 4
5) **1354** — G = 1, O = 3, L = 5, D = 4
6) **LOAD** — L = 5, O = 3, A = 2, D = 4
7) **6754** — P = 6, O = 7, L = 5, E = 4
8) **2513** — S = 2, L = 5, A = 1, Y = 3
9) **OPAL** — O = 7, P = 6, A = 1, L = 5
10) **7246** — F = 7, A = 2, R = 4, M = 6
11) **6132** — M = 6, E = 1, G = 3, A = 2
12) **BEAR** — B = 5, E = 1, A = 2, R = 4

Page 42 — Explore the Facts

1) **Jake** — Jake gets four toppings: sprinkles, chocolate sauce, raspberries and chopped nuts.

2) **Valeria** — Valeria draws two vegetables: cabbages and onions.

3) **Ferne** — Ferne competes in six events: the hammer throw, javelin throw, shot put, high jump, discus and hurdles.

4) **Robbie** — Robbie collects five different things: pinecones, wildflowers, leaves, sticks and acorns.

Page 43 — Explore the Facts

1) **Kia** — Kia likes three types of breakfast food: porridge, cereal and one other breakfast food.

2) **Skye** — Skye orders at least four ingredients: cheese, onion, red pepper, plus ham and/or tomato.

3) **Beth** — Beth reads nine pages: three pages of 'Space Secrets', four pages of 'Sunshine in Paris', one page of 'Dragon Diaries' and one page of 'Circus Mania'.

4) **Charlie** — Charlie had two hot meals last week: a beef burger on Friday and chicken pie on either Monday or Wednesday.

Page 44 — Solve the Riddle

1) **D** — The shop opened at 9.00. Kelly arrived an hour before it opened, so she must have arrived at 8.00. If Sanjay arrived 15 minutes after Kelly, he must have arrived at 8.15. Fran joined the queue half an hour before Sanjay, so she arrived at 7.45. Will was the last to join the queue, 10 minutes before the shop opened, so he must have joined at 8.50. Patience was not the first or last to arrive, so she must have arrived at some point between 7.45 and 8.50.

2) **E** — There are five children. Each of them have three marbles, so there are fifteen marbles in total. The most common colour is red, so at least six marbles must be red. Jordan has three red marbles, but both Seb and Lucy have two blue and one yellow. This means Olivia and Saleem must have at least three red marbles between them. They both have one yellow, so as at least three of the four marbles we don't know the colour of must be red, only one of Saleem or Olivia's marbles could be blue. This means that Saleem cannot have two blue marbles.

3) **C** — Harley held his breath for 6.2 seconds and Max held his breath for 8.6 seconds. The longest breath hold was 3.2 seconds longer than the second longest. There's only a 2.4 second difference between Harley and Max's breath holds, and we know Kaya held her breath for shorter than Harley, so the longest breath hold must be at least 3.2 seconds higher than Max's. This means Max cannot have held his breath the longest, so Harley cannot have had the second longest breath hold.

Page 45 — Solve the Riddle

1) **E** — Rhys and Cillian have the longest gap of time between them getting on the bus so they must be first and last. Niamh gets on 20 mins after Cillian, so Cillian must get on first. Bea gets on at 8.02, and Matthew gets on 12 minutes before, so he must get on at 7.50. Niamh must get on later than 7.50 because Matthew is second to get on the bus and Cillian is first. Niamh gets on 20 minutes later than Cillian, so Cillian can't have got on the bus before 7.30.

2) **A** — Getting halfway up a wall is worth 5 points, and Ollie made it halfway up 6 walls, so Ollie scored at least 30 points. Everyone got to the top of at least 3 walls, and getting to the top is worth 10 points, so Ollie must have scored at least 60 points overall. However, as there are 10 walls and Ollie only got halfway up 6 walls, he could not have reached the top of more than 4 walls, which means he must have scored a maximum of 70 points. Meredith and Charlotte both got 50 points, which is less than Ollie. The winner had a score of 85, and Finn missed out on winning by 10 points, so he must have a score of 75. This also means Surya must be the winner, as no one else could have got 85 points. As Finn and Surya both scored more points than Ollie, and Meredith and Charlotte scored less, Ollie must have come third.

3) **B** — Verity was the only person who cycled less than 10 km, so she must have cycled the shortest distance. Callum cycled the second furthest. Keisha cycled 4 km further than Haitao, so Haitao can't have cycled the furthest. This means only Keisha or Jessica could have cycled the furthest distance, which was 22 km. If Keisha cycled the furthest she must have cycled 22 km, which means that Haitao must have cycled 18 km. Haitao cycled twice as far as Verity, so in this scenario Verity must have cycled 9 km. As Verity and Jessica cycled a combined distance of 28 km, in this scenario Jessica must have cycled 19 km, which is further than Haitao. This means Haitao has to have cycled the second shortest distance. Alternatively, if Jessica cycled the furthest she must have cycled 22 km, which means that Verity must have cycled 6 km as their combined distance was 28 km. As Haitao cycled twice as far as Verity, in this scenario he must have cycled 12 km and Keisha, who cycled 4 km further than him, must have cycled 16 km. This means Haitao has to have cycled the second shortest distance, regardless of whether Keisha or Jessica cycled the furthest.

Pages 46-51 — Assessment Test 1

1) **4615** — T = 4, O = 6, U = 1, R = 5
2) **2654** — P = 2, O = 6, R = 5, T = 4
3) **TRIO** — T = 4, R = 5, I = 3, O = 6
4) **2536** — B = 2, A = 5, S = 3, K = 6
5) **1463** — E = 1, L = 4, K = 6, S = 3
6) **KALE** — K = 6, A = 5, L = 4, E = 1
7) **demand   insist** — Both of these mean 'to forcefully request'.
8) **dilemma   quandary** — Both of these mean 'a difficult problem'.
9) **transient   fleeting** — Both of these mean 'lasting for a short time'.
10) **trite   unoriginal** — Both of these mean 'overused or lacking freshness'.
11) **advocate   support** — Both of these mean 'publicly recommend'.
12) **FU** — HS and LO are mirror pairs, where the two letters are an equal distance from the centre of the alphabet. L is 4 letters forward from H, so the answer is FU, because F is 4 letters forward from B and U is its mirror pair.
13) **GD** — The first letter in the pair moves back 4 letters, the second letter moves forward 6 letters.
14) **VR** — The first letter in the pair moves forward 8 letters, the second letter moves back 9 letters.
15) **HS** — The first letter in the pair moves back 7 letters, the second letter moves forward 6 letters.

16) **RV** — WD and PK are mirror pairs, where the two letters are an equal distance from the centre of the alphabet. The answer will be the mirror pairs for E and I, which are V and R, but the letters are reversed.

17) **mileage** — 'mileage' is the only word that can be made.

18) **birthstone** — 'birthstone' is the only word that can be made.

19) **foresight** — 'foresight' is the only word that can be made.

20) **panicking** — 'panicking' is the only word that can be made.

21) **flippant** — 'flippant' is the only word that can be made.

22) **rivalled** — 'rivalled' is the only word that can be made.

23) **carnation** — 'carnation' is the only word that can be made.

24) **pharmacy   bank** — The other three are all places for leisure.

25) **construct   overhaul** — The other three all mean 'to make stronger'.

26) **salt   salsa** — The other three are all spices.

27) **hip   shield** — The other three are all parts of a book.

28) **though   afterwards** — The other three are all prepositions.

29) **Francesco** — Francesco has been to five places: York, Cardiff, Brighton, Edinburgh and Oxford.

30) **Chloe** — Chloe finds 8 sea creatures: four sea snails, three mussels and one starfish.

31) **arbitrary   studied** — They are the closest synonyms of 'random' and 'deliberate'.

32) **viable   sparse** — They are the closest antonyms of 'implausible' and 'copious'.

33) **ink   petrol** — They are liquids that are loaded into a printer and a car to make them operate.

34) **aloof   affable** — They are the closest synonyms of 'distant' and 'friendly'.

35) **ring   field** — They are where boxing and cricket matches take place.

36) **acre** — Take letters 2 and 3 from the second word, followed by letters 2 and 1 from the first word.

37) **rota** — Take letter 4 from the first word, followed by letters 3 and 2 from the second word, and then letter 3 from the first word.

38) **palm** — Take letters 2 and 3 from the first word, followed by letter 1 from the second word, and then letter 4 from the first word.

39) **stir** — Take letters 4 and 3 from the first word, followed by letter 3 from the second word, and then letter 2 from the first word.

40) **raid** — Take letters 2 and 3 from the second word, followed by letters 3 and 4 from the first word.

41) **c** — The new words are 'disc', 'calf', 'chic' and 'curl'.

42) **d** — The new words are 'tad', 'deep', 'held' and 'daft'.

43) **f** — The new words are 'leaf', 'face', 'self' and 'font'.

44) **w** — The new words are 'show', 'wage', 'flaw' and 'wake'.

45) **k** — The new words are 'week', 'king', 'beak' and 'keel'.

46) **credible   untrustworthy** — 'credible' means 'able to be relied on as truthful', whereas 'untrustworthy' means 'not able to be relied on as truthful'.

47) **pacify   provoke** — 'pacify' means 'to restore calm', whereas 'provoke' means 'to stir up anger'.

48) **vindicate   disprove** — 'vindicate' means 'to show to be right or justified', whereas 'disprove' means 'to show to be false'.

49) **unassuming   conceited** — 'unassuming' means 'modest', whereas 'conceited' means 'vain'.

50) **notorious   illustrious** — 'notorious' means 'well-known, typically for something bad or disreputable', whereas 'illustrious' means 'well-known, respected and admired'.

51) **E** — 9 × 6 − 15 − 18 = 21, E = 21

52) **C** — 24 ÷ 8 + 12 − 3 = 12, C = 12

53) **D** — 4 × 8 − 25 + 12 = 19, D = 19

54) **A** — 25 ÷ 5 × 7 − 30 = 5, A = 5

55) **B** — 21 ÷ 7 × 9 − 18 = 9, B = 9

56) **E** — 5 × 12 − 22 − 16 = 22, E = 22

57) **area seems** — The hidden word is 'ease'.

58) **choir only** — The hidden word is 'iron'.

59) **together once** — The hidden word is 'hero'.

60) **able students** — The hidden word is 'lest'.

61) **orchid lecture** — The hidden word is 'idle'.

62) **c** — The new words are 'both' and 'pact'.

63) **i** — The new words are 'plan' and 'hoist'.

64) **d** — The new words are 'boar' and 'body'.

65) **i** — The new words are 'sold' and 'wiry'.

66) **f** — The new words are 'deer' and 'left'.

67) **ZB** — The first letter in each pair moves in the sequence -4, +3, -4, +3, -4. The second letter in each pair moves forward 5 letters each time.

68) **OR** — The first letter moves in the sequence -2, -1, O, +1, +2. The second letter moves forward 3 letters each time.

69) **RY** — The first letter moves in the sequence -2, -4, -6, -8, -10. The second letter moves in the sequence +3, +5, +7, +9, +11.

70) **MJ** — The first letter in each pair moves in the sequence -6, +3, -6, +3, -6. The second letter in each pair moves in the sequence +3, +4, +5, +6, +7.

71) **HU** — The first letter moves in the sequence +2, +1, O, -1, -2. The second letter moves in the sequence -1, O, +1, +2, +3.

72) **C** — Adnan finished in 2 minutes 28 seconds. Chris finished in half this time, so he finished in 1 minute 14 seconds. There were 1.5 seconds between Rory and Chris, and Rory reached the end before him, so Rory must have finished in 1 minute 12.5 seconds. The fastest time was 1 minute 12 seconds, so Rory can't be first. This means only Suki or Courtney can be first. If Suki and Adnan finish in the same time, 2 minutes 28 seconds, this means Courtney would have to come first and Suki and Adnan would be last. However, Suki wasn't last, so Adnan and Suki cannot have finished in the same time.

73) **E** — Brayden doesn't have maple syrup. Amara ends up with sugar, strawberries and bananas, so she doesn't have maple syrup either. Uriah has the same toppings as Amara, minus the strawberries, so he also doesn't have maple syrup. Joey and Willow both have maple syrup on their pancakes, so only two people have maple syrup. Joey and Amara both have strawberries, but Uriah doesn't. We know that Brayden has more toppings than Uriah, who has two toppings, so Brayden must have three: strawberries, bananas and sugar (because he doesn't have maple syrup). Willow doesn't eat fruit, so three people have strawberries. Willow doesn't have bananas, but Amara, Uriah and Brayden do, so three people have bananas. Amara, Uriah and Brayden also all have sugar. We don't know whether Willow has sugar, but at least three people do. This means that maple syrup must be the least popular topping.

74) **2** — The number subtracted doubles each time: -2, -4, -8, -16.

75) **6** — There are two sequences which alternate. In the first you divide by 2 each time, and in the second you multiply by 4 each time.

76) **360** — Multiply by descending numbers: ×5, ×4, ×3, ×2, ×1.

77) **71** — The number added halves each time: +32, +16, +8, +4, +2, +1.

78) **14** — There are two sequences which alternate. In the first you subtract 6 each time, and in the second you multiply by 3 each time.

79) **5** — Subtract square numbers in ascending order: -4, -9, -16, -25, -36.

80) **79** — Add prime numbers in descending order: +19, +17, +13, +11, +7.

Pages 52-57 — Assessment Test 2

1) **stubborn** — 'stubborn' is the only word that can be made.

2) **rearrange** — 'rearrange' is the only word that can be made.

3) **bursting** — 'bursting' is the only word that can be made.

4) **asphalt** — 'asphalt' is the only word that can be made.

5) **sincerely** — 'sincerely' is the only word that can be made.

6) **3152** — O = 3, R = 1, E = 5, S = 2

7) **2346** — S = 2, O = 3, F = 4, T = 6

8) **TOES** — T = 6, O = 3, E = 5, S = 2

9) **6542** — R = 6, E = 5, N = 4, D = 2

10) **7145** — T = 7, O = 1, N = 4, E = 5

11) **IRON** — I = 3, R = 6, O = 1, N = 4

12) **plot** — 'plot' can mean 'conspiracy' or 'a small area of land'.

13) **deduction** — 'deduction' can mean 'a decision reached by reasoning' or 'an amount that is taken away'.

14) **legion** — 'legion' can mean 'very large in number' or 'a large group of people'.

15) **cape** — 'cape' can mean 'a large piece of land jutting out into water' or 'a sleeveless cloak'.

Answers

16) **fetter** — 'fetter' can mean 'a chain used to restrain a prisoner' or 'to prevent someone from doing something'.

17) **GLFGH** — This is a mirror code, where each letter is an equal distance from the centre of the alphabet. T is 7 letters forward from the centre, and G is 7 letters back; O is 2 letters forward and L is 2 letters back; U is 8 letters forward and F is 8 letters back; T is 7 letters forward and G is 7 letters back; S is 6 letters forward and H is 6 letters back.

18) **PRISM** — To get from the code to the word move the letters in the sequence -1, +2, -3, +4, -5.

19) **ROAST** — To get from the code to the word move the letters in the sequence +1, -1, -3, -5, -7.

20) **FMPCW** — To get from the word to the code move the letters in the sequence +3, -2, +3, -2, +3.

21) **ONRKRZ** — To get from the word to the code move the letters in the sequence -4, -2, O, +2, +4, +6.

22) **YEARS** — To get from the code to the word move the letters in the sequence −3, +3, -2, +2, -1.

23) **BRIGHT** —To get from the code to the word move the letters in the sequence +2, -1, O, +2, -1, O.

24) **blood** — The first letter of the word moves forward one place along the alphabet. The last letter of the word moves backwards two places along the alphabet.

25) **oil** — Rearrange letters 2, 4, 8 in the order 4, 2, 8.

26) **par** — Rearrange letters 2, 6, 7 in the order 2, 7, 6.

27) **ten** — Rearrange letters 2, 3, 10 in the order 10, 3, 2.

28) **eon** — Rearrange letters 5, 8, 10 in the order 10, 8, 5.

29) **extra cheese** — The hidden word is 'ache'.

30) **New homes** — The hidden word is 'whom'.

31) **flew down** — The hidden word is 'lewd'.

32) **some reason** — The hidden word is 'mere'.

33) **losing library** — The hidden word is 'glib'.

34) **y** — The new words are 'fort' and 'flying'.

35) **g** — The new words are 'land' and 'bang'.

36) **o** — The new words are 'spilt' and 'orate'.

37) **e** — The new words are 'corps' and 'piety'.

38) **g** — The new words are 'resin' and 'dirge'.

39) **2** — Add the two outer numbers together (5 + 7 = 12). Divide the answer by 6 (12 ÷ 6 = 2).

40) **36** — Subtract the third number from the first number (13 − 4 = 9). Multiply the answer by the third number (9 × 4 = 36).

41) **18** — Divide the first number by the third number (80 ÷ 8 = 10). Multiply the answer by 2 (10 × 2 = 20). Subtract 2 (20 − 2 = 18).

42) **6** — Add the two outer numbers together (6 + 18 = 24). Divide the answer by 4 (24 ÷ 4 = 6).

43) **9** — Subtract the first number from the third number (22 − 19 = 3). Square the answer (3 × 3 = 9).

44) **17** — Multiply the two outer numbers (4 × 2 = 8). Multiply the answer by 2 (8 × 2 = 16). Add 1 (16 + 1 = 17).

45) **C** — Four of Rana's shots were saved, and she missed the goal five times, so Rana must have scored her remaining 3 penalties. Eve scored more than half her penalties, so she must have scored between 7 and 12 penalties. Eve scored twice as many penalties as Marcel, so Eve must have scored 8, 10 or 12 penalties, and Marcel must have scored 4, 5 or 6. Marcel scored two more penalties than Hasim, so Hasim scored a maximum of 4 penalties. Hasim and Christian scored 7 penalties between them, so Christian scored at least 3 penalties. Therefore, Rana can't have scored more penalties than Christian.

46) **B** — Sujatha was the first to arrive and was early, so she arrived at 1.59 pm at the latest. The last person arrived 35 minutes after her. Landon arrived at 2.25 pm and Mei arrived after him, so the earliest Sujatha could have arrived was 1.51 pm. Darren arrived 20 minutes after Sujatha, so he arrived between 2.11 pm and 2.19 pm. Mei arrived after Landon, so she must have arrived after 2.25 pm, so Darren must have arrived before Mei.

47) **2** — 6 × 11 ÷ 3 − 14 = 8, 8 = 48 ÷ 8 + 2

48) **3** — 72 ÷ 8 + 23 − 17 = 15, 15 = 72 ÷ 6 + 3

49) **10** — 63 ÷ 9 × 4 − 19 = 9, 9 = 10 × 3 − 21

50) **5** — 5 × 12 ÷ 4 + 34 = 49, 49 = 11 × 5 − 6

51) **9** — 11 × 9 ÷ 3 − 15 + 43 = 61, 61 = 9 × 5 + 16

52) **11** — 132 ÷ 11 × 7 − 18 + 55 = 121, 121 = 99 ÷ 9 × 11

53) **7** — 54 ÷ 6 × 9 − 17 + 8 = 72, 72 = 42 ÷ 7 × 12

54) **53** — The numbers follow the sequence +18, +12, +6, O, -6.

55) **27** — There are two sequences which alternate. In the first, the number is multiplied by 3 each time. In the second, the number is multiplied by 12 each time.

56) **105** — Multiply by descending odd numbers: ×7, ×5, ×3, ×1.

57) **209** — The two previous numbers are added together to get the next number in the sequence.

58) **30** — There are two sequences which alternate. In the first, the number is multiplied by ascending odd numbers: ×1, ×3, ×5. In the second, the number is divided by descending even numbers: ÷4, ÷2.

59) **tentative categorical** — 'tentative' means 'not certain', whereas 'categorical' means 'absolutely certain'.

60) **imperceptible palpable** — 'imperceptible' means 'impossible to see', whereas 'palpable' means 'plain to see'.

61) **anomalous typical** — 'anomalous' means 'not customary', whereas 'typical' means 'customary'.

62) **conjecture certitude** — 'conjecture' means 'speculation', whereas 'certitude' means 'certainty'.

63) **despondency euphoria** — 'despondency' means 'great sadness', whereas 'euphoria' means 'great joy'.

64) **Gav** — Gav watches four acts: 'Land of Noise', 'Soundburst', 'Blue Tigers' and 'Bandit Boys'.

65) **Tara** — Tara does three activities: mountain biking, kayaking and canyoning.

66) **BIT** — The complete word is HABITAT.

67) **DIG** — The complete word is INDIGNANT.

68) **LEG** — The complete word is ILLEGIBLE.

69) **ACE** — The complete word is ADJACENT.

70) **SEE** — The complete word is BESEECH.

71) **contain grip** — They are the main purposes of a 'pail' and 'tongs'.

72) **unsavoury lukewarm** — They are antonyms of 'delectable' and 'ardent'.

73) **food sunlight** — They are what someone is lacking if they are emaciated or pasty.

74) **leather clothes** — They are what a tanner and a tailor make.

75) **canyon river** — They are larger versions of a ravine and a stream.

76) **YJ** — The first letter in the pair moves in the sequence -1, O, +1, +2, +3. The second letter moves back 1 letter then forward 3 letters alternately.

77) **KM** — The first letter in the pair moves in the sequence -8, -6, -4, -2, O. The second letter moves forward 6 letters then forward 3 letters alternately.

78) **AV** — The first letter in the pair moves forward 3 letters then forward 4 letters alternately. The second letter moves in the sequence +2, +6, +10, +14, +18.

79) **UA** — The first letter in the pair moves in the sequence +8, +3, -2, -7, -12. The second letter moves back five letters then forward 6 letters alternately.

80) **MM** — The first letter in the pair moves forward 5 letters then back 9 letters alternately. The second letter moves in the sequence +11, +7, +3, -1, -5.

Pages 58-63 — Assessment Test 3

1) **7** — 96 ÷ 8 + 73 − 27 + 16 = 74, 74 = 9 × 9 − 7

2) **12** — 8 × 9 ÷ 6 + 47 − 21 = 38, 38 = 132 ÷ 12 + 27

3) **10** — 108 ÷ 9 × 3 + 18 + 57 = 111, 111 = 10 × 9 + 21

4) **4** — 56 ÷ 7 × 11 + 97 − 72 = 113, 113 = 24 × 4 + 17

5) **19** — 12 × 12 ÷ 8 + 77 − 38 = 57, 57 = 19 × 4 − 19

6) **w** — The new words are 'claw', 'warn', 'slow' and 'wear'.

7) **e** — The new words are 'floe', 'ear', 'shoe' and 'each'.

8) **m** — The new words are 'helm', 'malt', 'seam' and 'mark'.

9) **g** — The new words are 'glug', 'gout', 'ping' and 'gist'.

10) **o** — The new words are 'too', 'oust', 'hero' and 'oil'.

11) **D** — 69 ÷ 23 × 3 × 8 − 69 + 20 = 23, D = 23

12) **E** — 5 × 12 ÷ 30 × 22 − 2 − 12 = 30, E = 30

13) **C** — 8 × 9 ÷ 6 × 3 − 22 − 6 = 8, C = 8

14) **A** — 6 × 4 × 5 ÷ 12 + 12 − 18 = 4, A = 4

15) **B** — 8 × 6 ÷ 12 × 9 − 25 + 6 − 9 = 8, B = 8

16) **is leaving** — The hidden word is 'isle'.

17) **Global meat** — The hidden word is 'balm'.

18) **everyone else** — The hidden word is 'eels'.

19) **maze always** — The hidden word is 'zeal'.

20) **stop using** — The hidden word is 'opus'.

21) **most** — Take letters 2 and 3 from the second word, followed by letters 5 and 3 from the first word.

22) **tall** — Take letters 5 and 3 from the second word, followed by letter 3 from the first word, then letter 2 from the second word.

23) **grow** — Take letter 3 from the second word, followed by letters 5 and 3 from the first word, then letter 1 from the second word.

24) **onus** — Take letter 2 from the second word, followed by letters 2 and 1 from the first word, then letter 5 from the second word.

25) **tuba** — Take letter 4 from the first word, followed by letter 2 from the second word, then letter 1 from the first word, then letter 5 from the second word.

26) **RAW** — The complete word is FARAWAY.

27) **ANT** — The complete word is MANTLE.

28) **LAG** — The complete word is PILLAGED.

29) **MEN** — The complete word is AMENITY.

30) **ROW** — The complete word is PROWESS.

31) **6512** — V = 6, E = 5, S = 1, T = 2

32) **3145** — I = 3, S = 1, L = 4, E = 5

33) **SILT** — S = 1, I = 3, L = 4, T = 2

34) **4367** — O = 4, M = 3, I = 6, T = 7

35) **5671** — S = 5, I = 6, T = 7, E = 1

36) **TONS** — T = 7, O = 4, N = 2, S = 5

37) **sully soil** — Both of these mean 'to make dirty'.

38) **defeatist pessimistic** — Both of these mean 'believing the worst will happen'.

39) **bestow confer** — Both of these mean 'to present an honour'.

40) **shrewdness acumen** — Both of these mean 'the ability to make good judgements'.

41) **seminal influential** — Both of these mean 'being of great influence'.

42) **2** — Divide by descending numbers: ÷9, ÷7, ÷5, ÷3.

43) **19** — Subtract descending square numbers: -49, -36, -25, -16, -9.

44) **54** — There are two sequences which alternate. In the first sequence, the numbers follow the sequence +5, +7, +9. In the second sequence, subtract 3 each time.

45) **145** — Add ascending prime numbers: +19, +23, +29, +31, +37.

46) **228** — Add descending cube numbers: +125, +64, +27, +8, +1.

47) **OP** — The first letter in the pair moves forward 11 letters, the second letter moves back 4 letters.

48) **BW** — FU and IR are mirror pairs, where the two letters are an equal distance from the centre of the alphabet. The answer will be the mirror pairs for D and Y, which are W and B, but the letters are reversed.

49) **AT** — The first letter in the pair moves back 10 letters, the second letter moves back 8 letters.

50) **NW** — The first letter in the pair moves forward 12 letters, the second letter moves back 11 letters.

51) **TG** — QJ, HS and CX are mirror pairs, where the two letters are an equal distance from the centre of the alphabet. H is 9 letters back from Q, so the missing mirror pair is TG, because T is 9 letters back from C, and G is its mirror pair.

52) **impressionist protagonist** — The other three are all professions.

53) **thwart furnish** — The other three all mean 'to load heavily'.

54) **surgery infirmary** — The other three are all places of safety and shelter.

55) **flexible dispensable** — The other three all mean 'easily influenced'.

56) **whale shark** — The other three are all invertebrates (animals which don't have a backbone).

57) **FLINT** — This is a mirror code, where each letter is an equal distance from the centre of the alphabet. U is 8 letters forward from the centre, and F is 8 letters back; O is 2 letters forward and L is 2 letters back; R is 5 letters forward and I is 5 letters back; M is 1 letter back and N is 1 letter forward; G is 7 letters back and T is 7 letters forward.

58) **WRRIB** — To get from the word to the code move the letters in the sequence -5, -3, -1, +1, +3.

59) **BOOST** — To get from the code to the word move the letters in the sequence -2, +2, -3, +3, -4.

60) **EDIBLE** — To get from the code to the word move the letters in the sequence +6, +4, +2, O, -2, -4.

61) **QTFUEV** — To get from the word to the code move the letters in the sequence -2, +4, -3, +3, -4, +2.

62) **Amad** — Amad watched 4 plays: 'Hamlet', 'Othello', 'Twelfth Night' and 'Macbeth'.

63) **Millie** — Millie visited 2 exhibits: Ancient Egypt and the Romans.

64) **pilot** — 'pilot' can mean 'control the movement of' or 'a test done before introducing a new thing'.

65) **speculate** — 'speculate' can mean 'to take a risk' or 'to make guesses about something'.

66) **appropriate** — 'appropriate' can mean 'suitable or relevant' or 'to take something without permission'.

67) **accent** — 'accent' can mean 'a distinctive way of pronouncing words' or 'a distinct emphasis'.

68) **negotiate** — 'negotiate' can mean 'to try to reach an agreement with someone' or 'to find a way through'

69) **4** — Find the midpoint of the two outer numbers (26 + 30 = 56) (56 ÷ 2 = 28). Divide the answer by 7 (28 ÷ 7 = 4).

70) **15** — Divide the first number by the third number (25 ÷ 5 = 5). Multiply the answer by 3 (5 × 3 = 15).

71) **10** — Add the two outer numbers together (11 + 13 = 24). Divide the answer by 3 (24 ÷ 3 = 8). Add 2 (8 + 2 = 10).

72) **32** — Multiply the two outer numbers (9 × 8 = 72). Subtract the third number from the answer (72 − 8 = 64). Halve the answer (64 ÷ 2 = 32).

73) **7** — Subtract the first number from the third number (8 − 6 = 2). Multiply the answer by the first number (2 × 6 = 12). Subtract 5 (12 − 5 = 7).

74) **cot** — Remove letters 3, 4, 5, 6, 7 and 9 leaving the remaining letters in the order 1, 2, 8.

75) **ray** — Remove letters 1, 3, 5, 6, 7 and 8, leaving the remaining letters in the order 2, 4, 9.

76) **see** — Remove letters 1, 2, 4, 5, 6 and 9, leaving the remaining letters in the order 3, 7, 8.

77) **not** — Rearrange letters 3, 5, 8 in the order 8, 5, 3.

78) **men** — Rearrange letters 1, 3, 10 in the order 3, 10, 1.

79) **D** — Patrick got 38 hours' sleep, and Eniola had the least sleep, so she must have had fewer than 38 hours' sleep. Keith slept for 3 hours more than Eniola, so he must have had fewer than 41 hours' sleep. Sasha slept for 9 hours on Monday to Wednesday, and at least 7 hours on Thursday and Friday, so she must have had at least 41 hours' sleep over the five nights. Therefore, Sasha must have got more sleep than Keith.

80) **B** — Alex scored twice as many points as Gwen, so if Alex scored 160 points, Gwen would have scored 80 points. Everyone hit the bullseye at least once, so Gwen scored at least 50 points from hitting the bullseye. For Gwen to have a final score of 80 points, she would have needed to score 30 more points. However, each shot that hit the target outside of the bullseye was worth 20 points, so it is not possible that Gwen scored 80 points in total. This means Alex cannot have scored 160 points.

Progress Chart

Use this chart to keep track of your scores for the Assessment Tests.

You can do each test more than once — download extra answer sheets from cgpbooks.co.uk/11plus/answer-sheets or scan the QR code on the right.

Answer Sheets

	First Go	Second Go	Third Go
Test 1	Date: Score:	Date: Score:	Date: Score:
Test 2	Date: Score:	Date: Score:	Date: Score:
Test 3	Date: Score:	Date: Score:	Date: Score:

Look back at your scores once you've done all the Assessment Tests.

Each test is out of 80 marks.

Work out which kind of mark you scored most often:

0-43 marks — Keep working on it. These questions are designed to stretch you.

44-63 marks — You're doing great! These questions are really tricky.

64-80 marks — Wow! You're a Verbal Reasoning star.